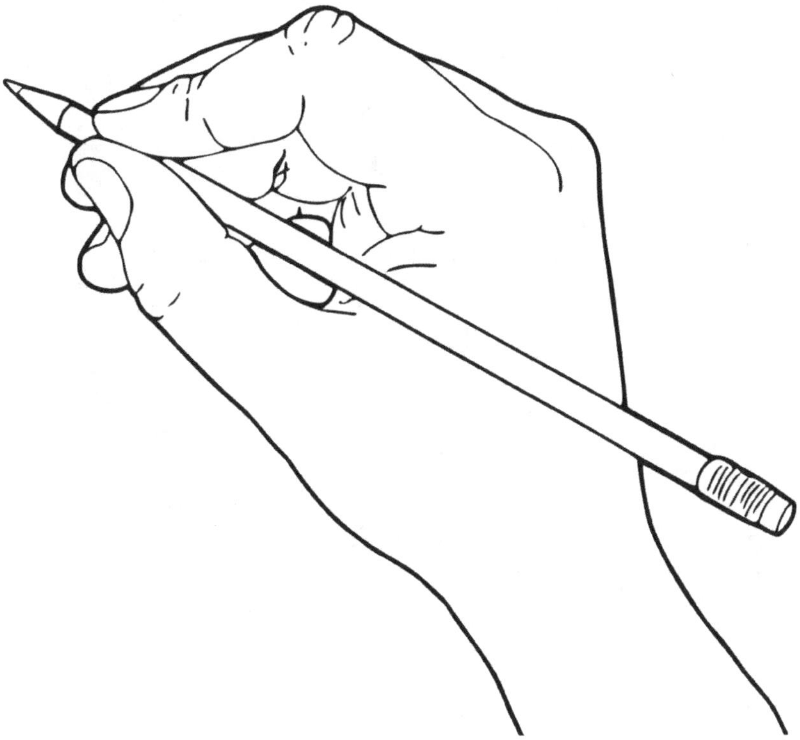

This Notebook belongs to:

____

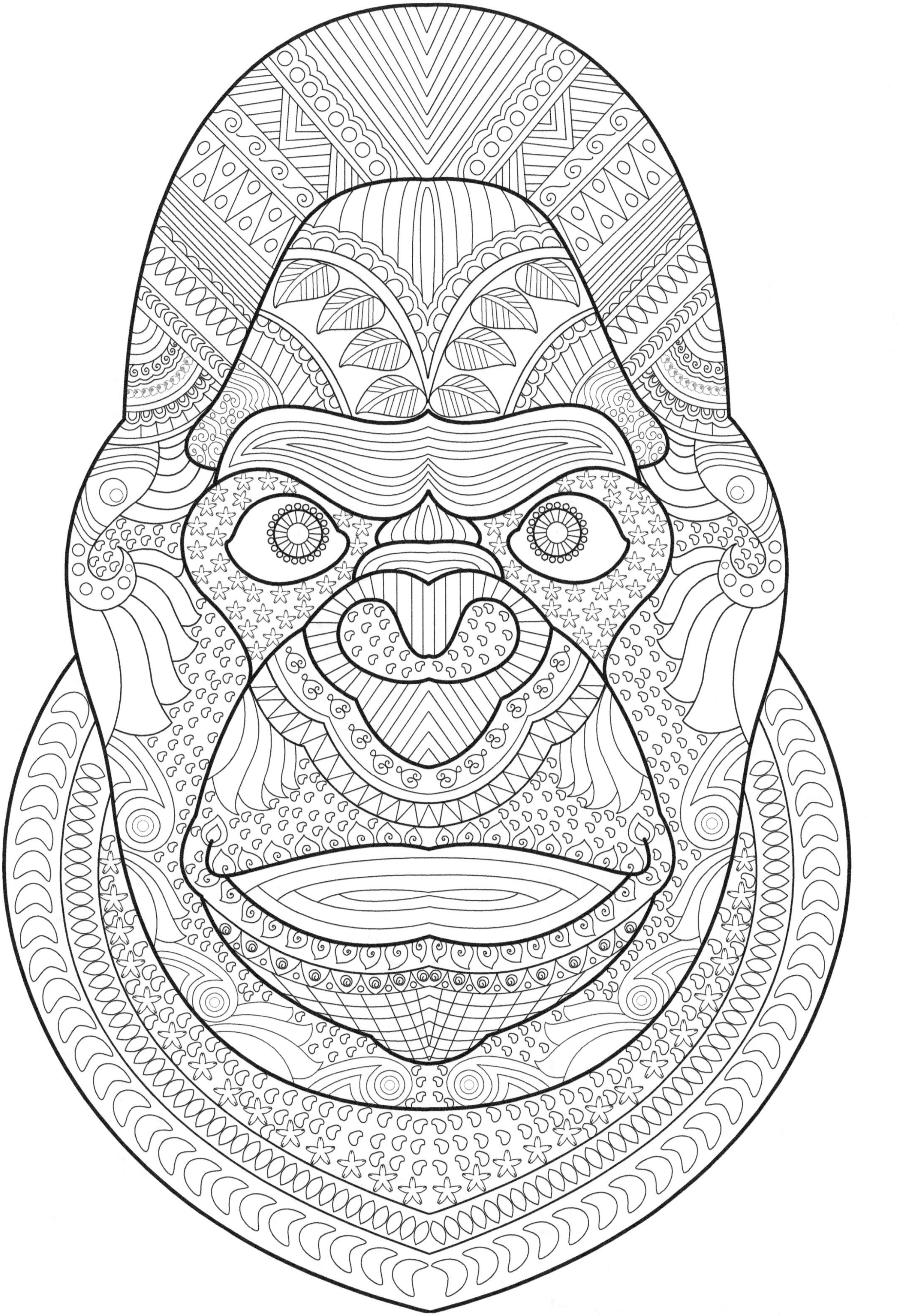

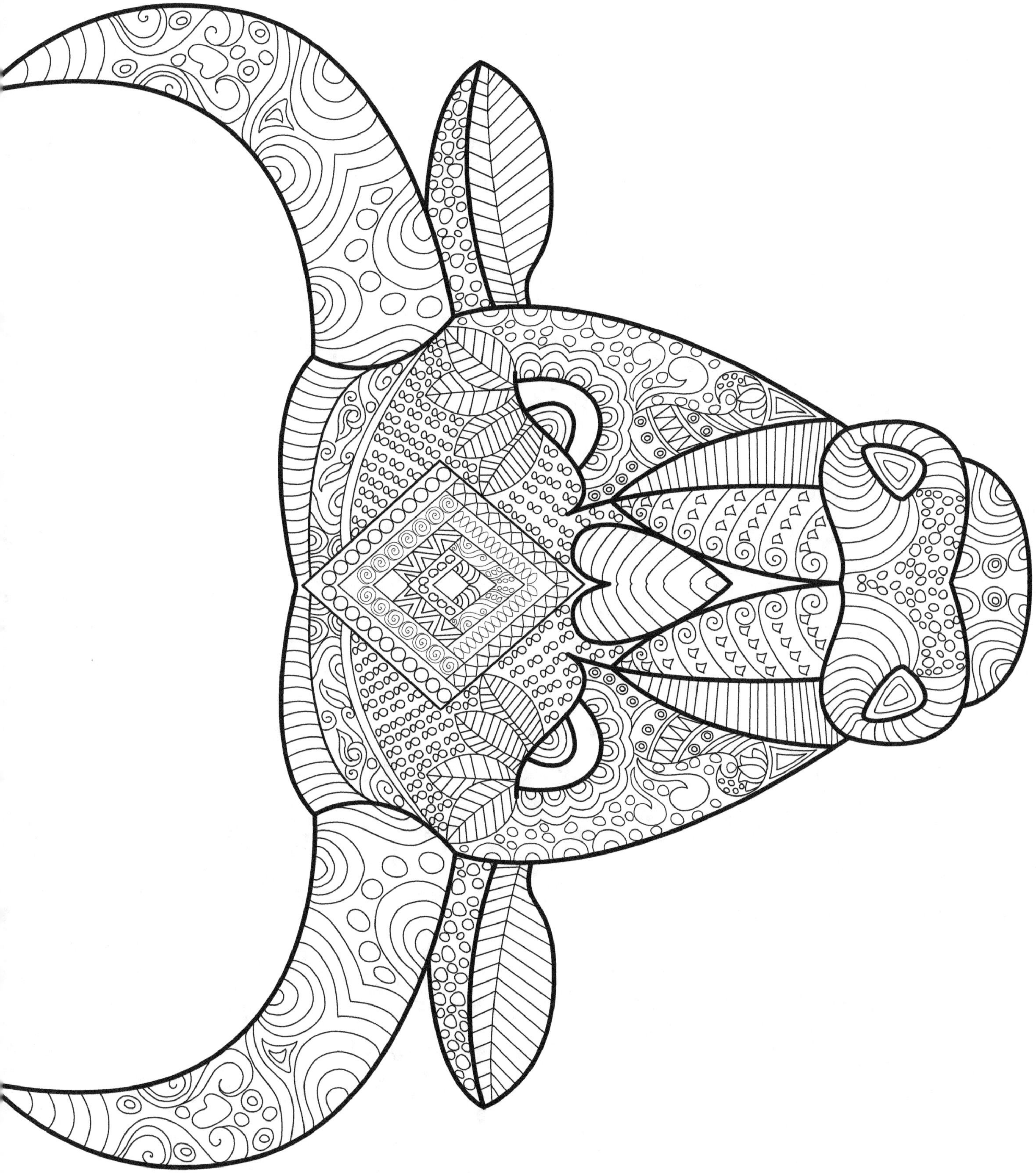

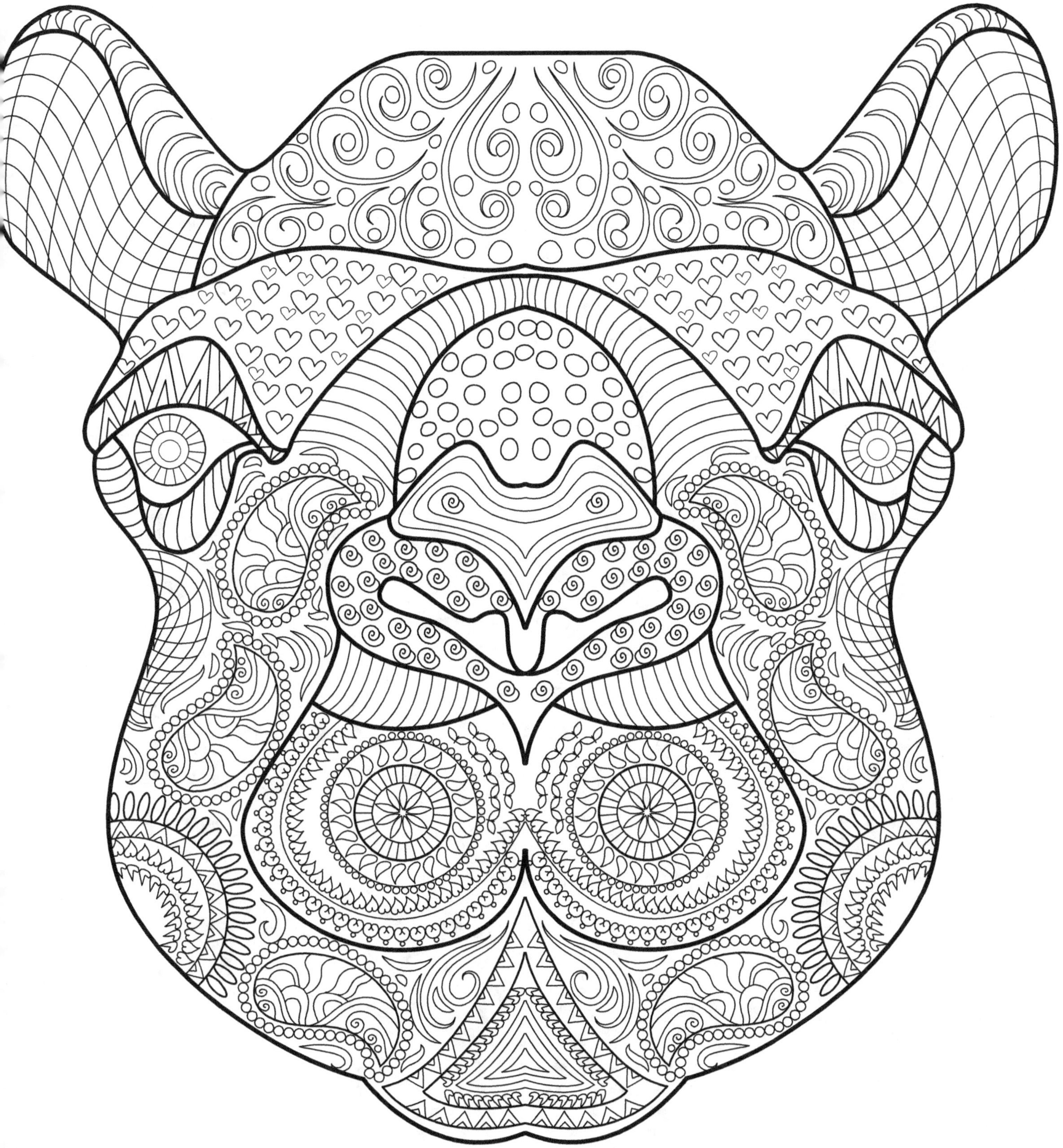

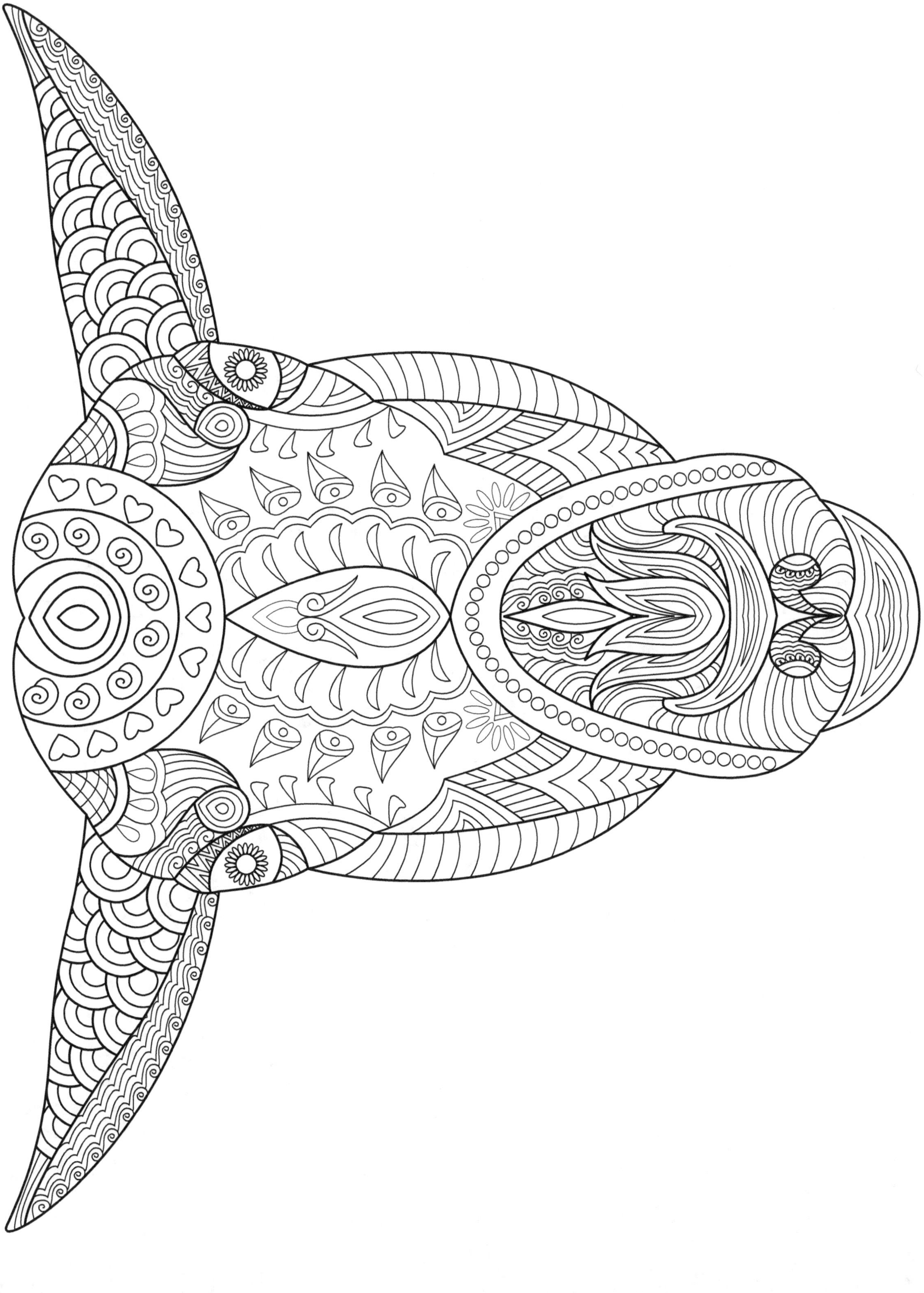

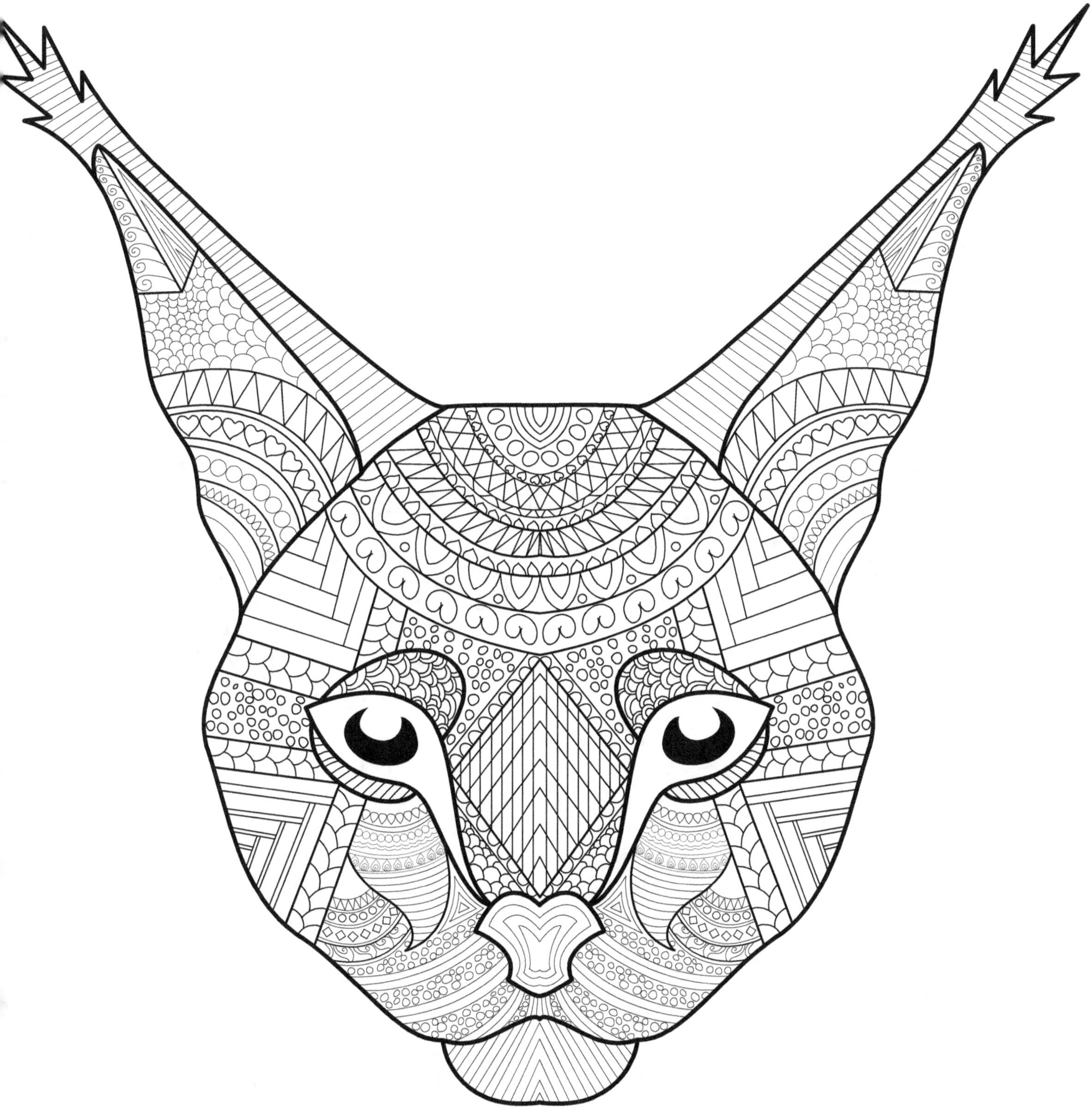

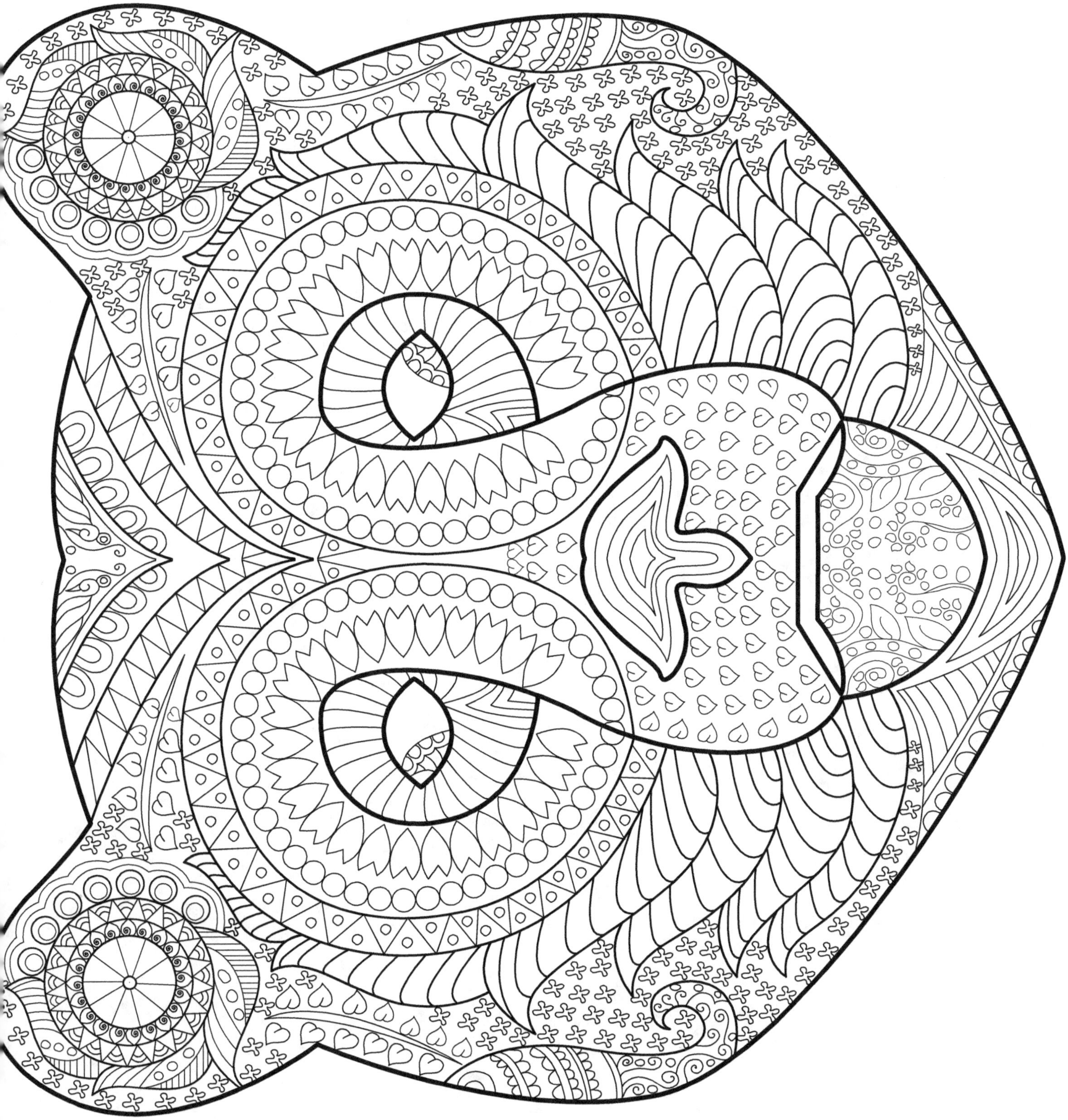

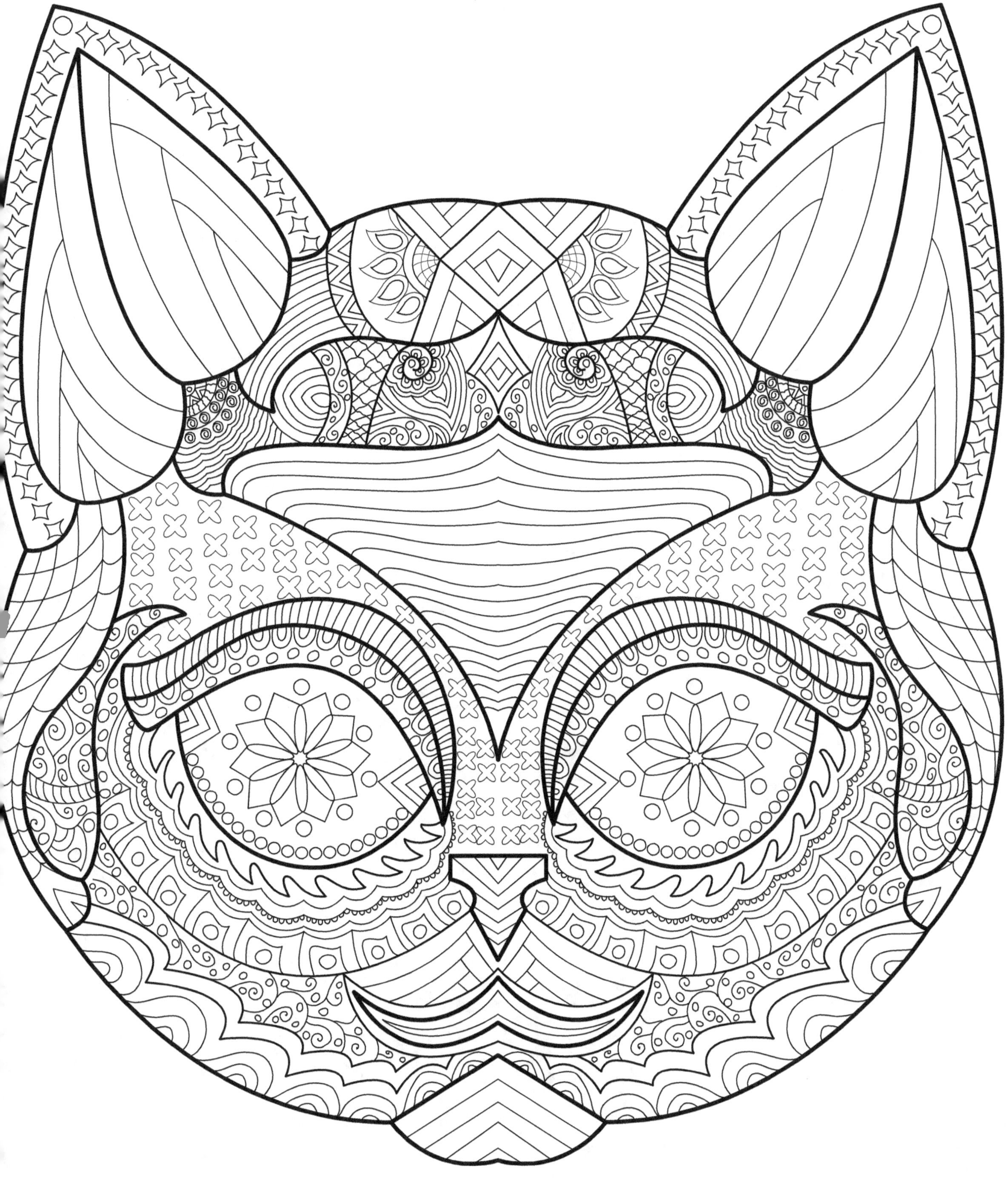

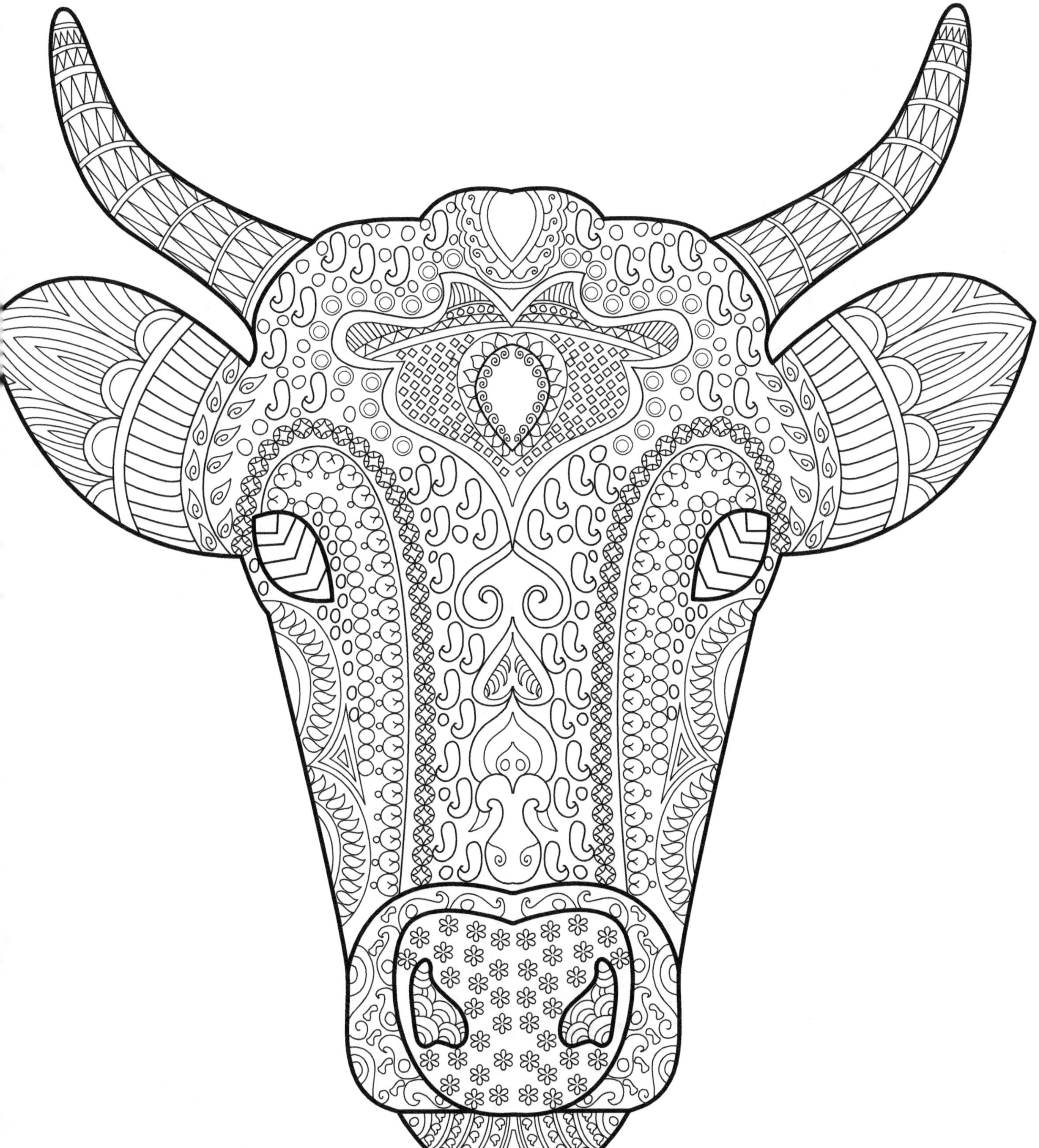

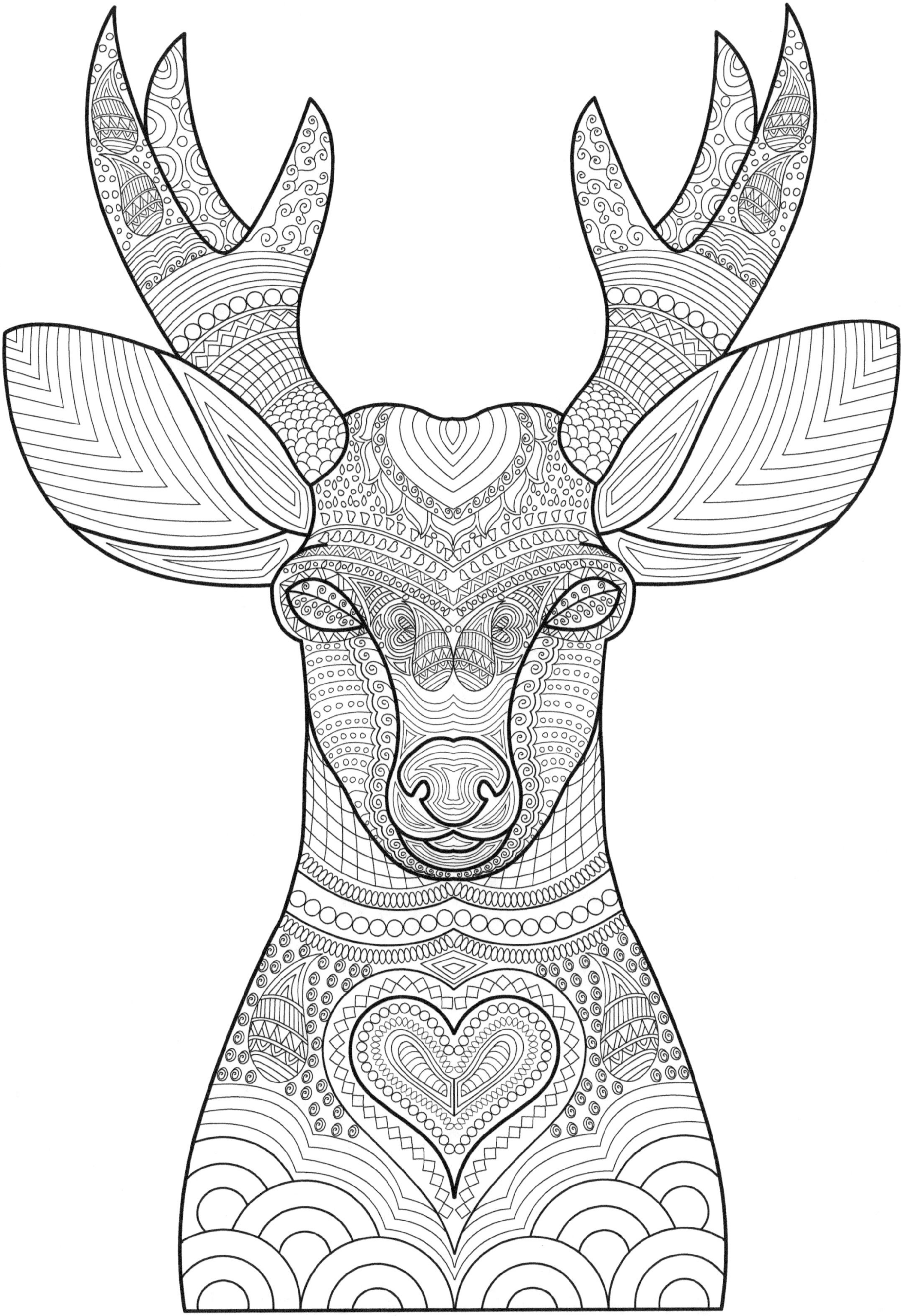

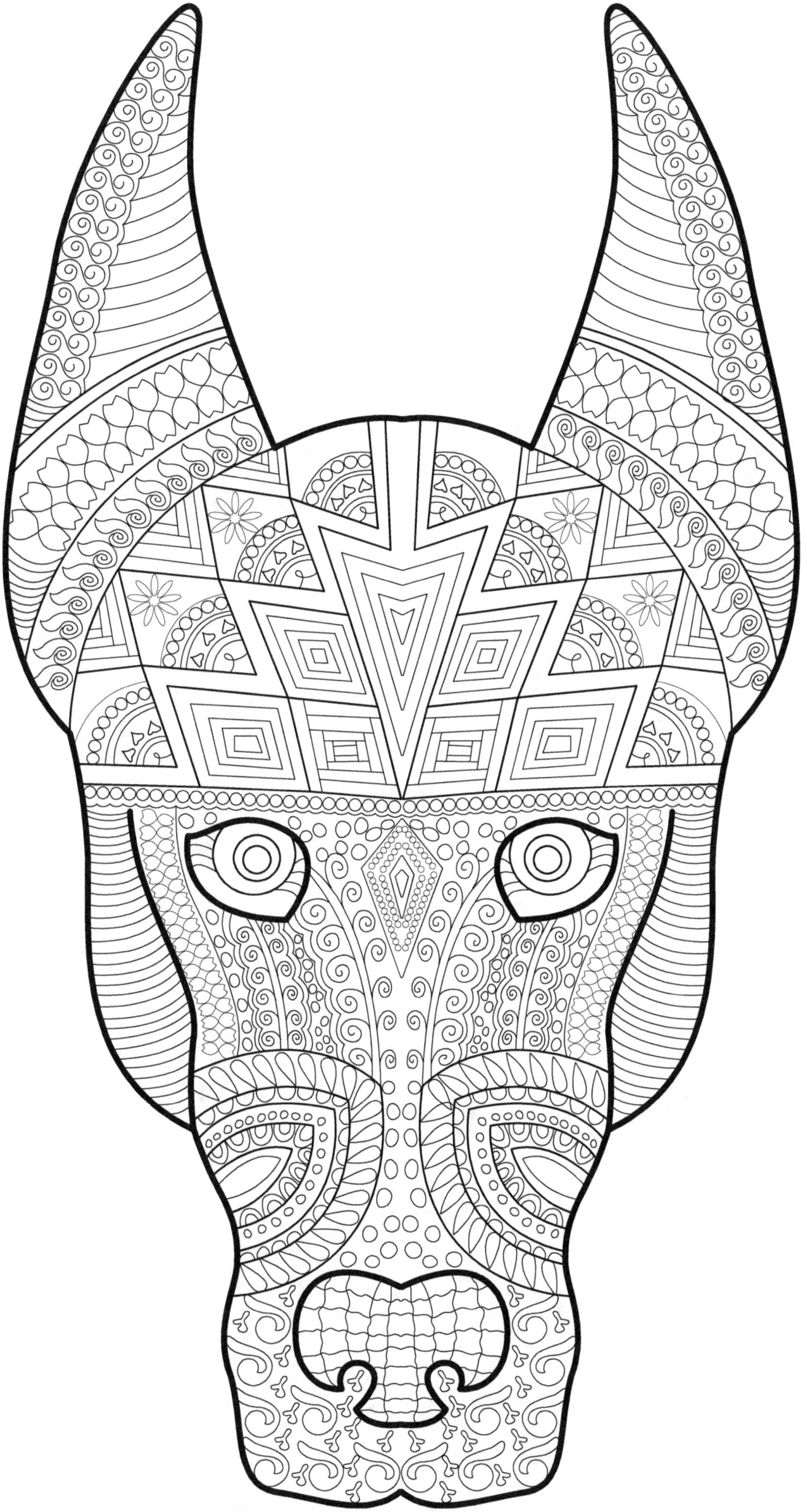

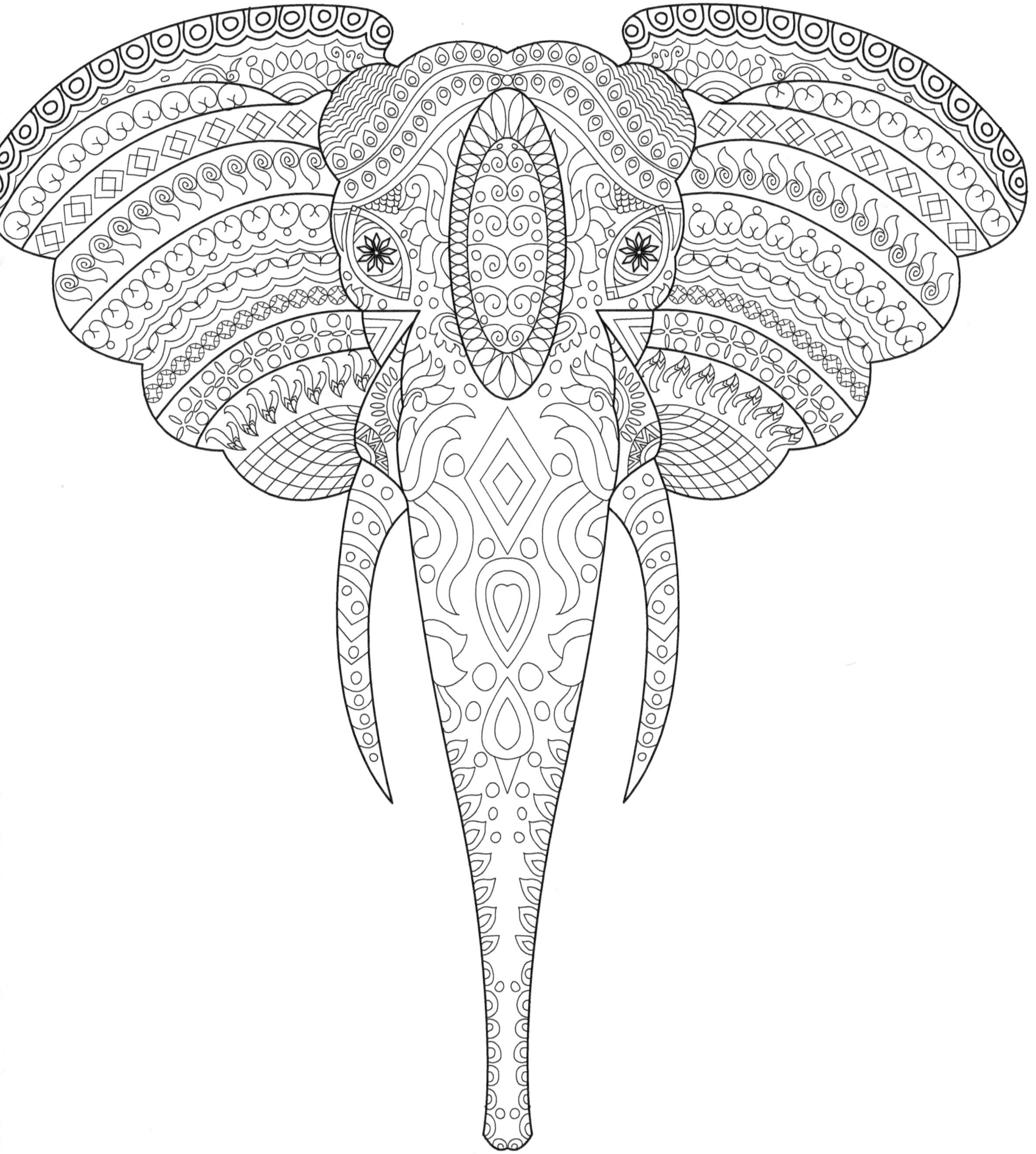

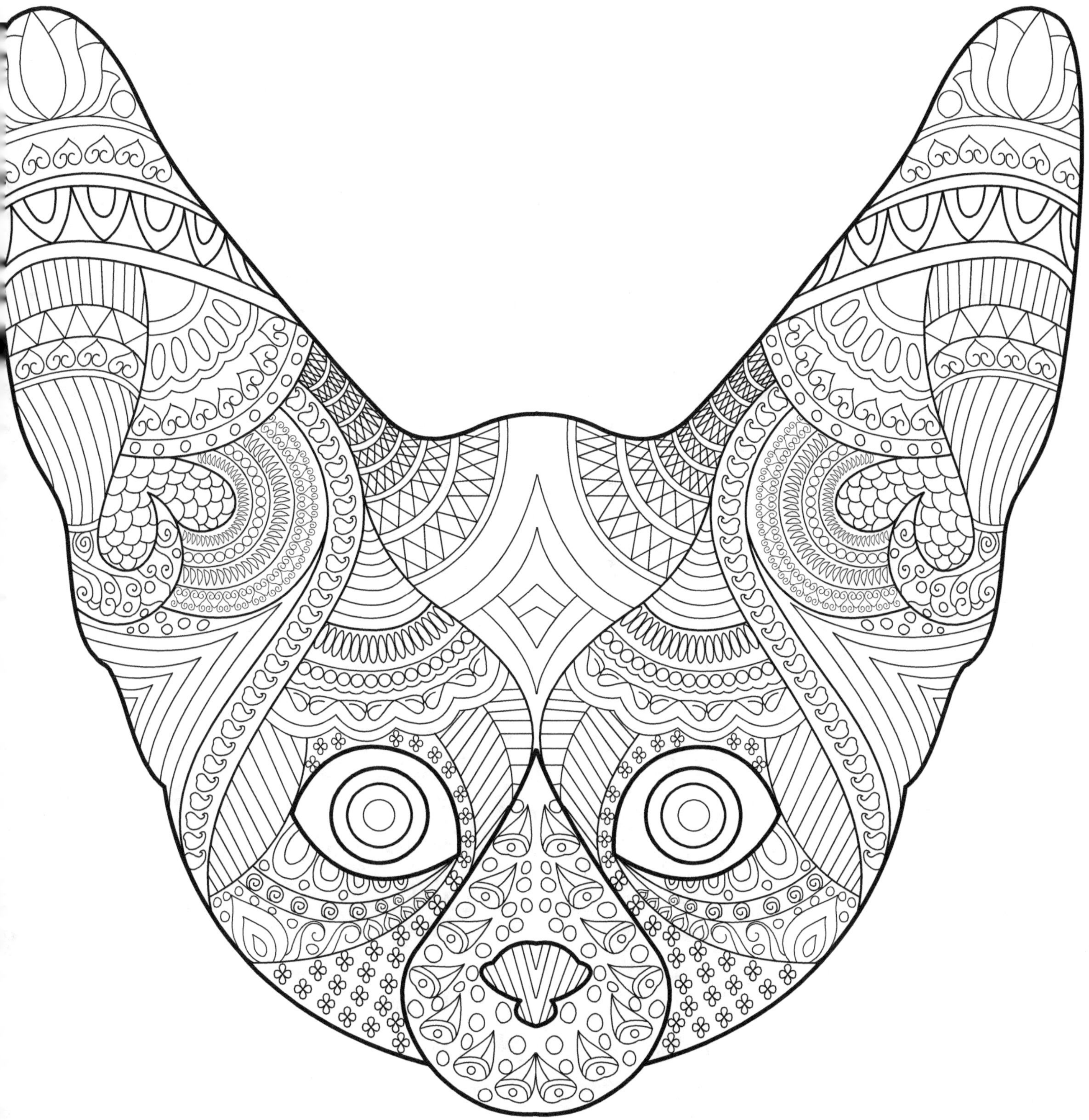

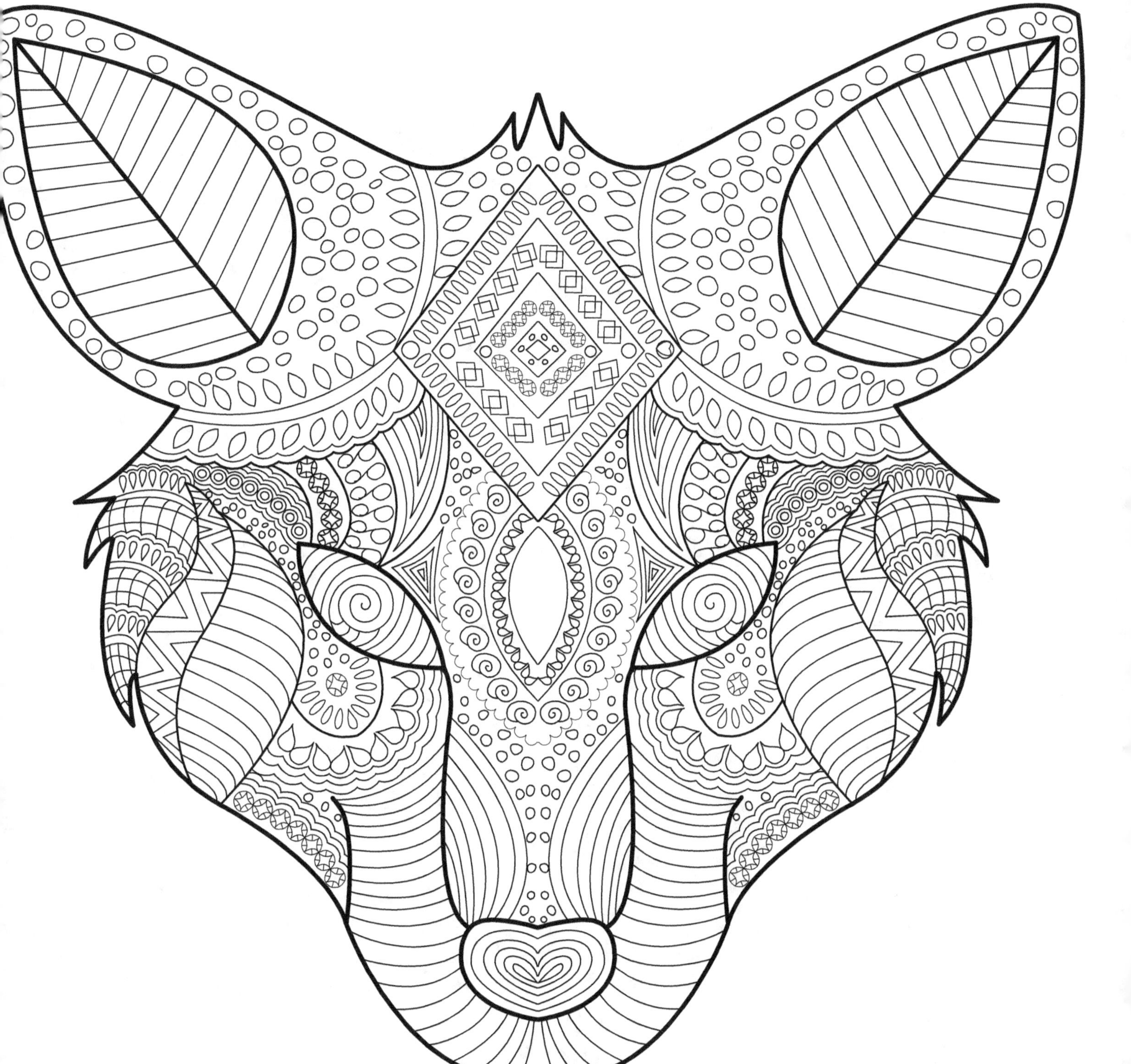

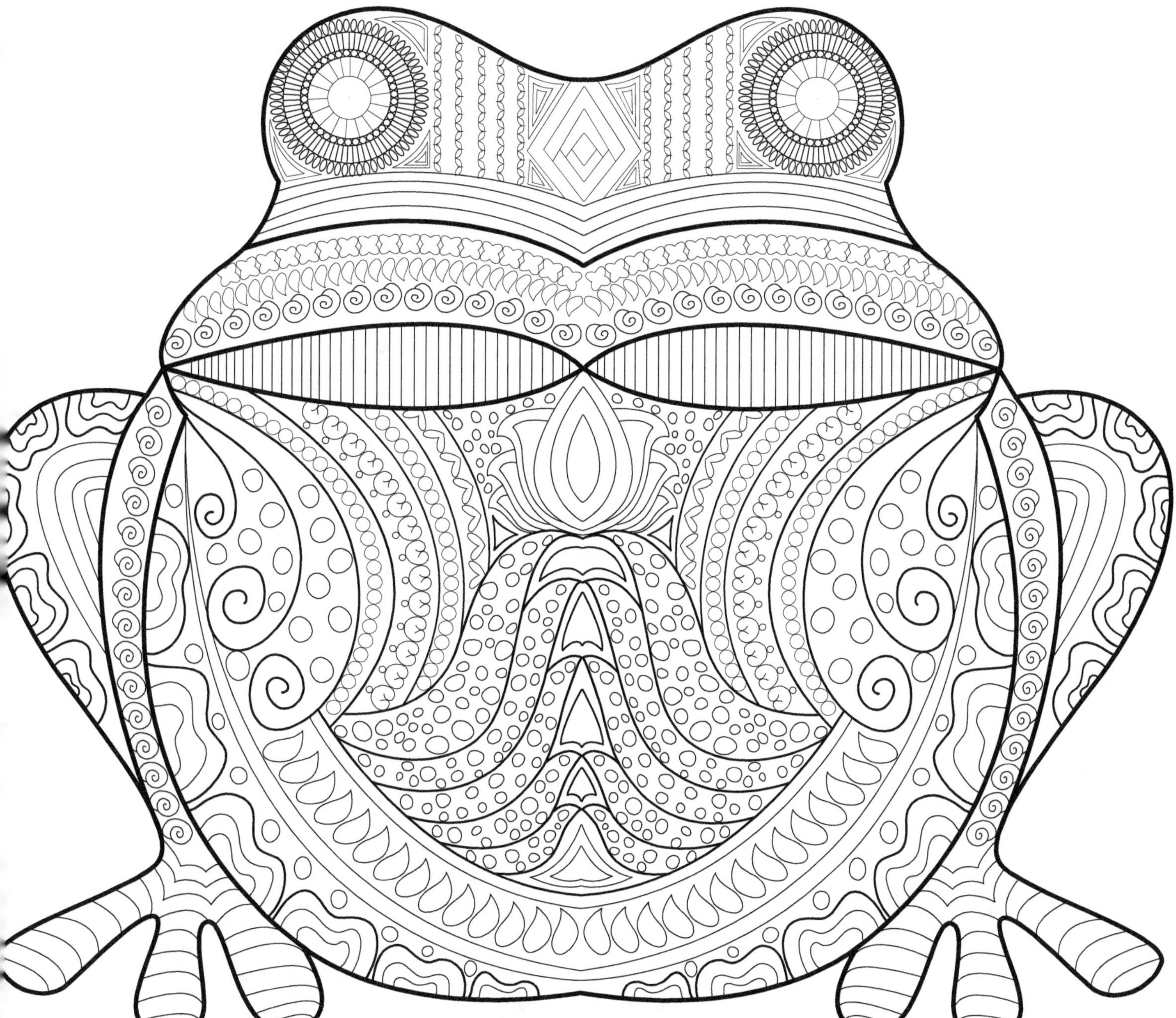

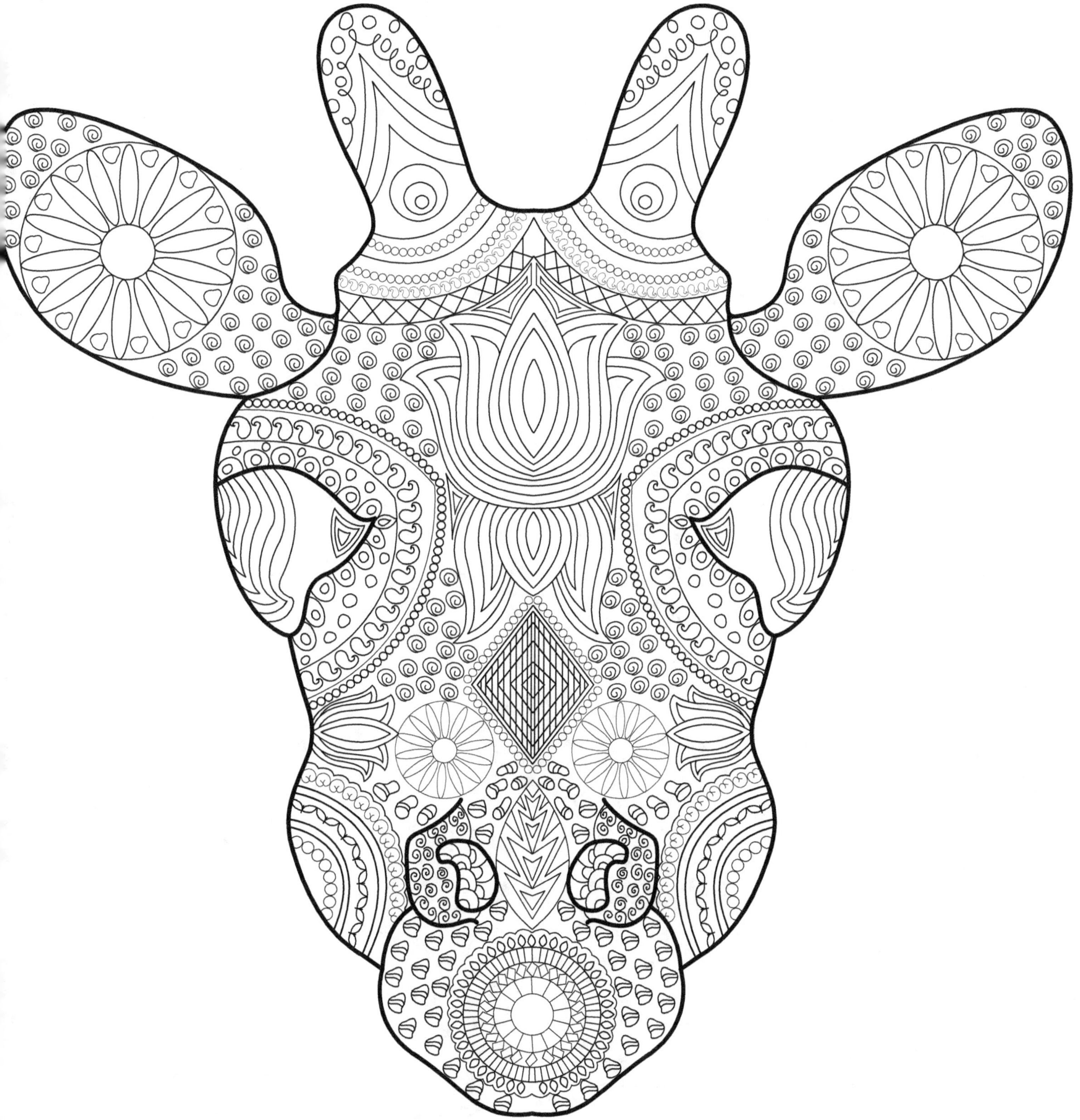

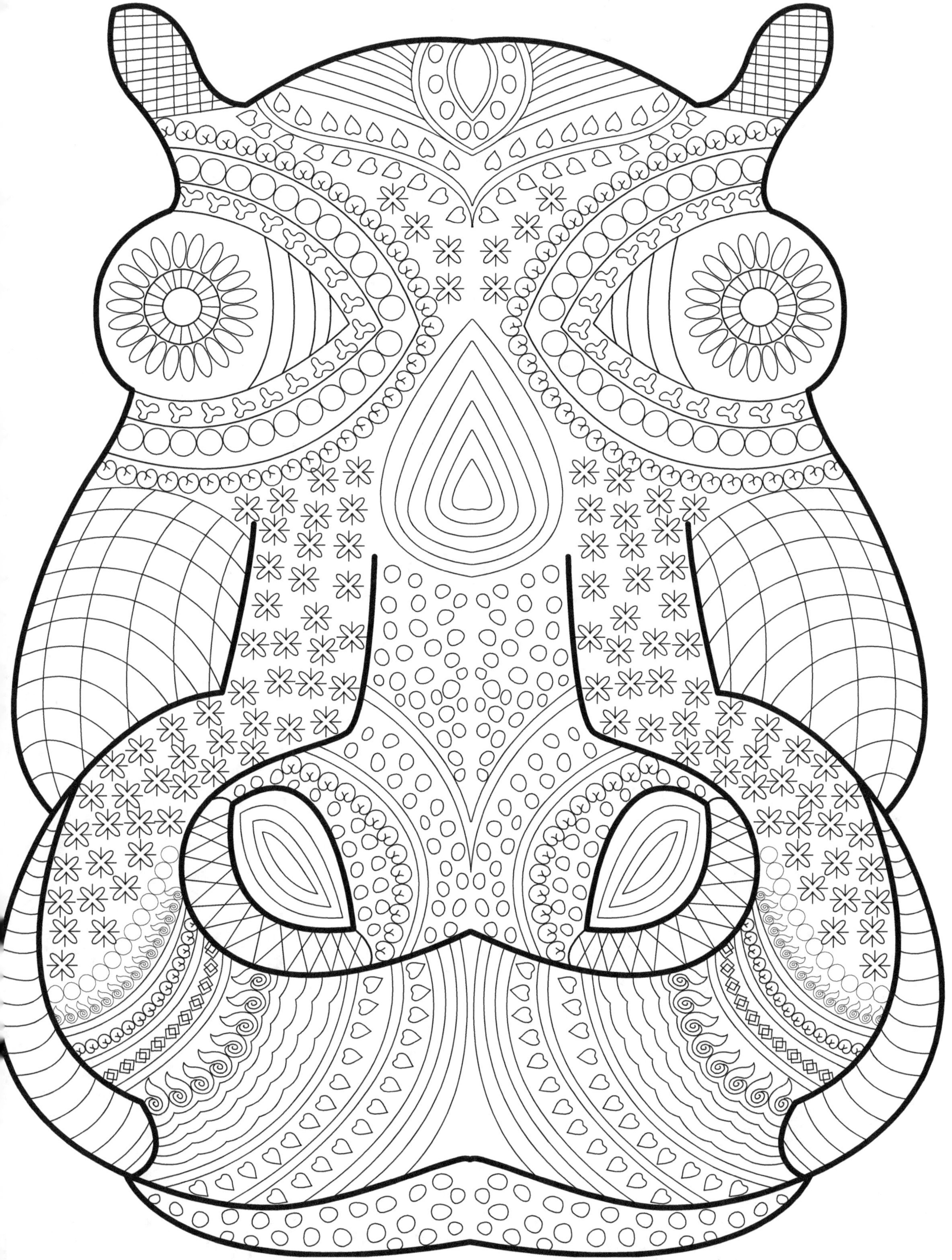

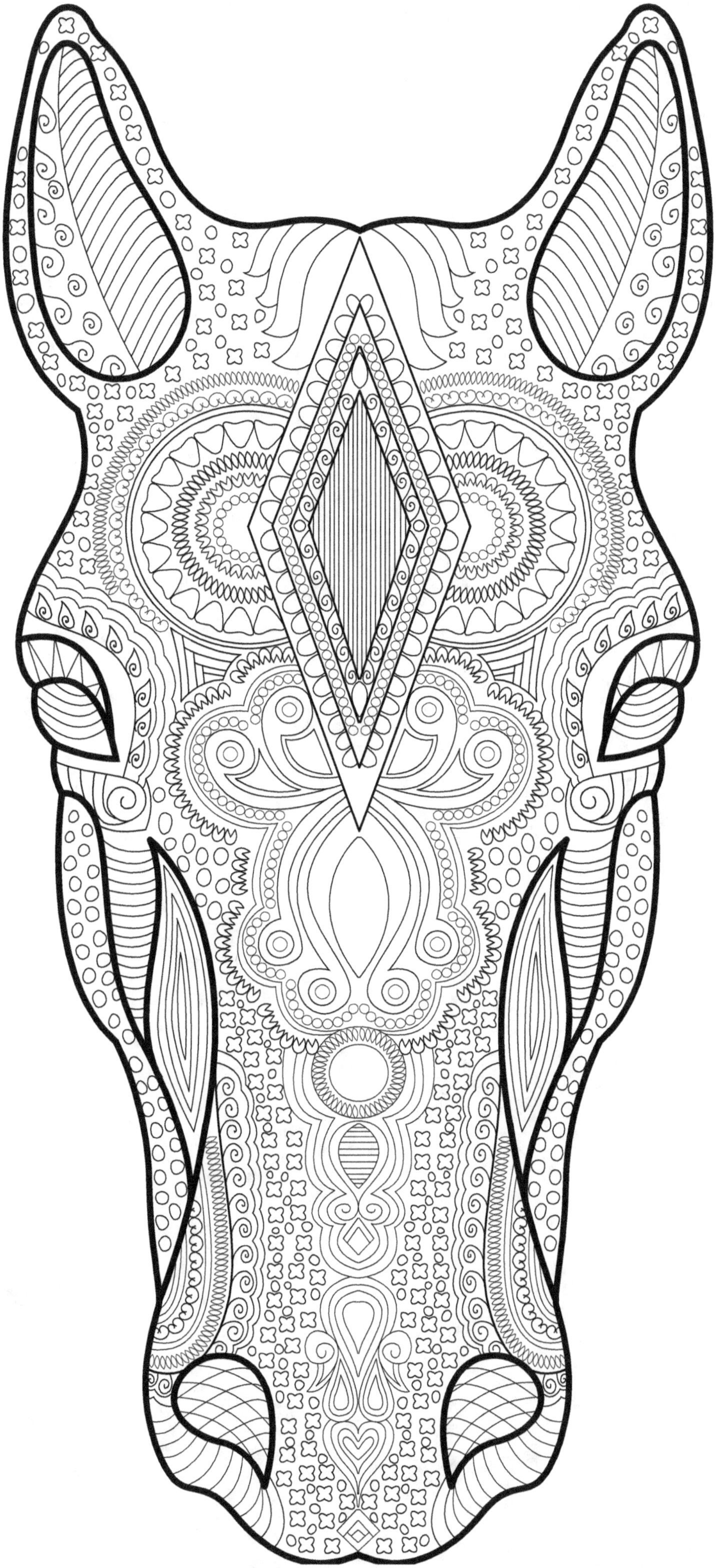

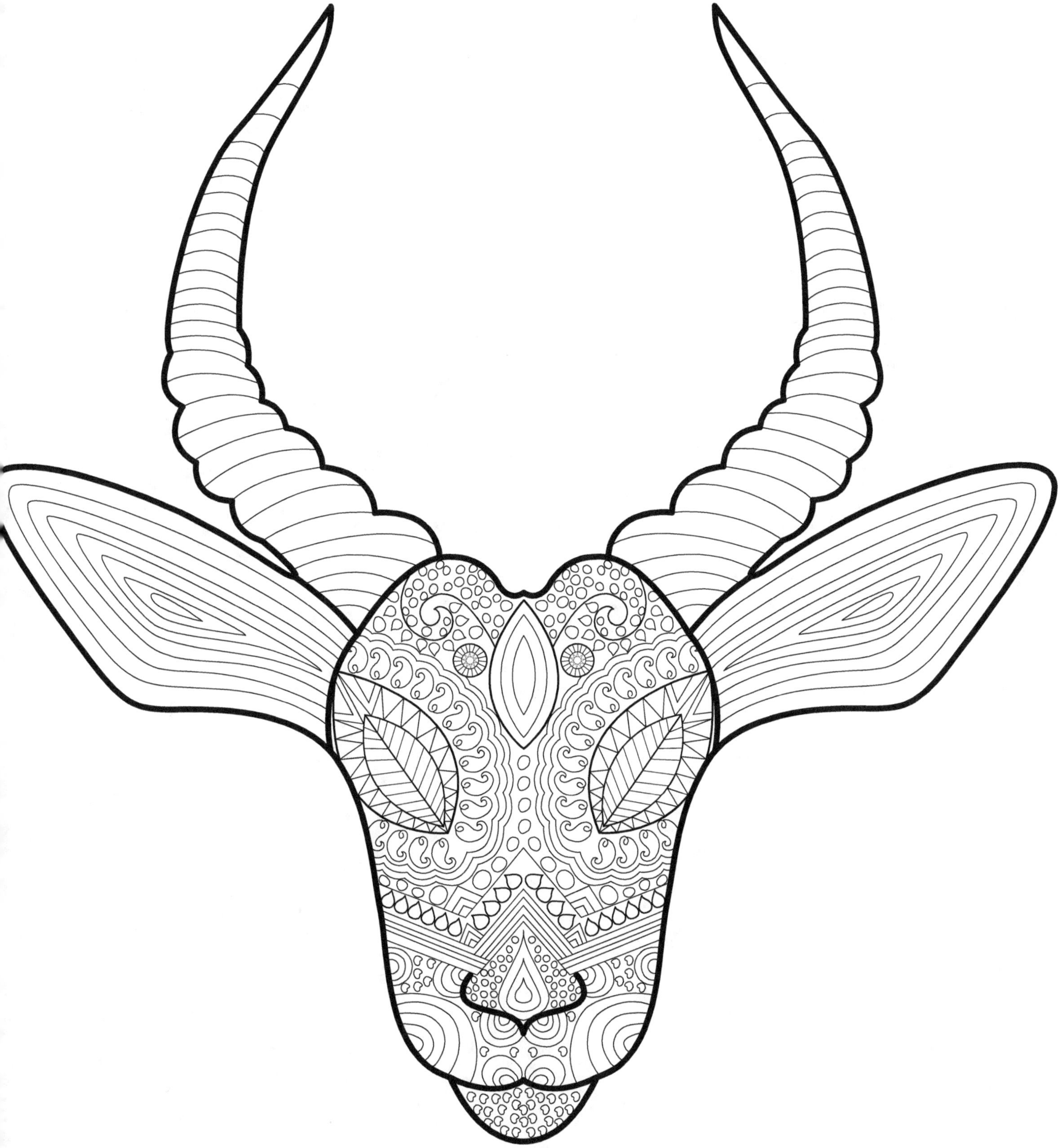

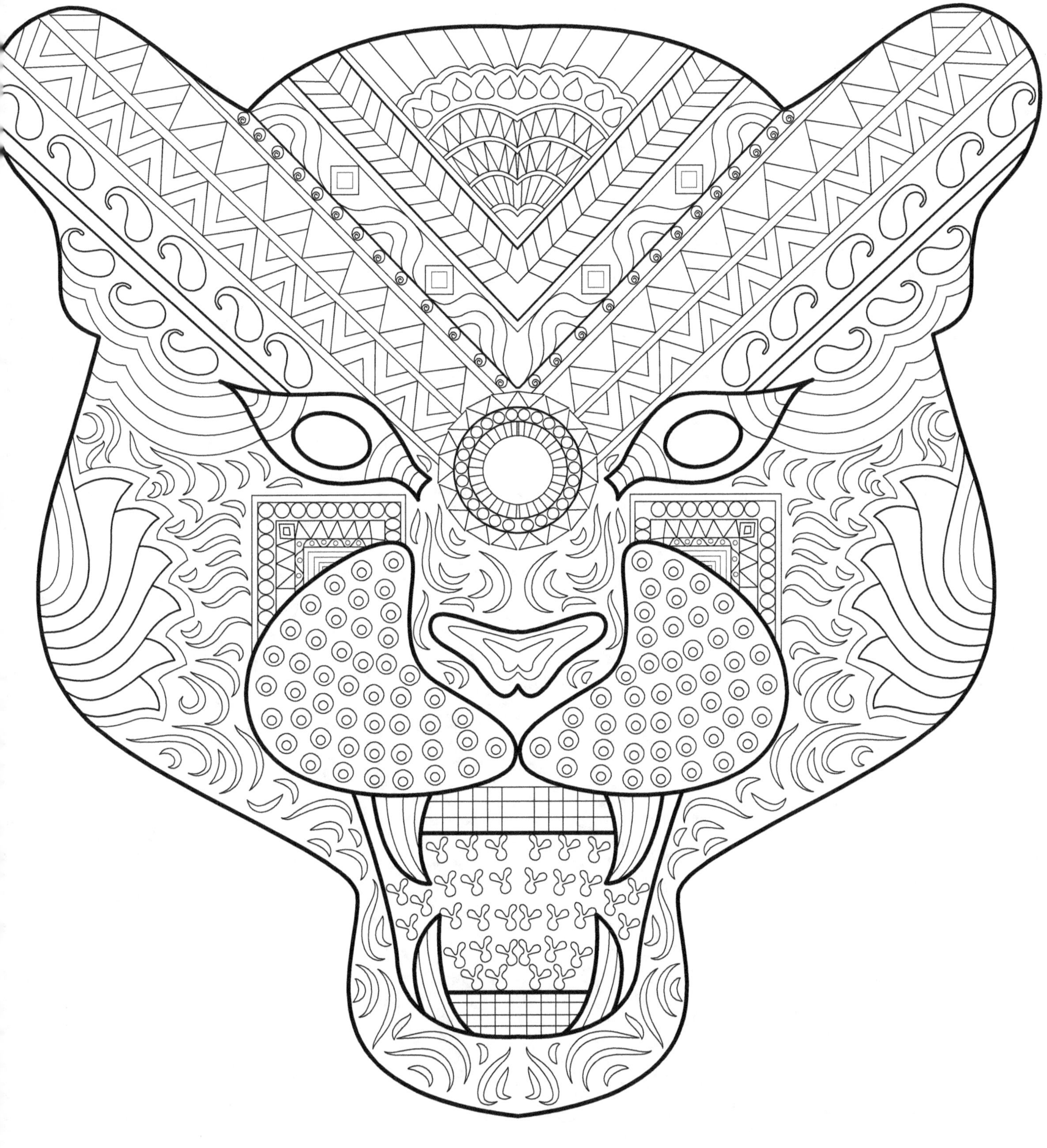

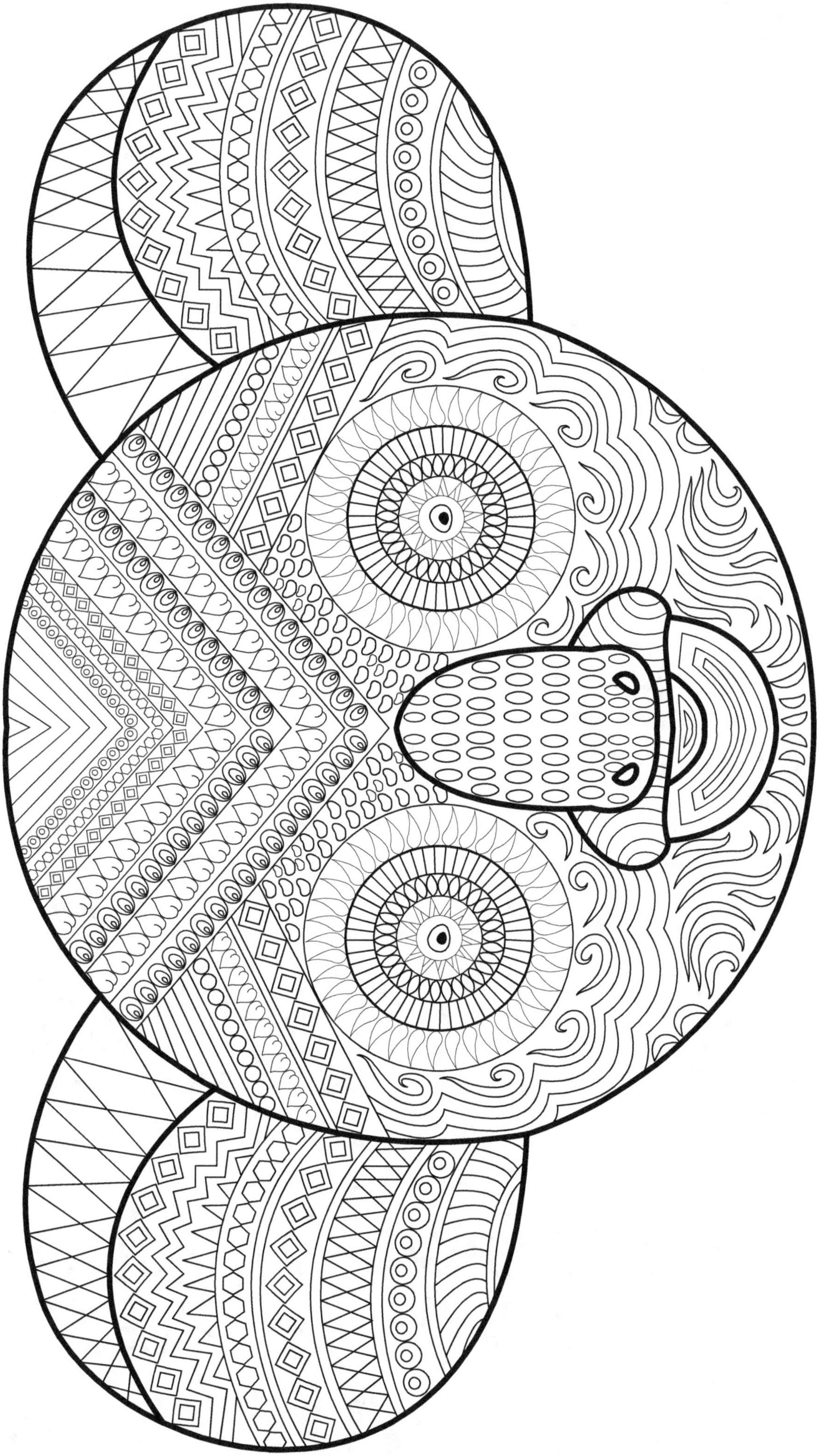

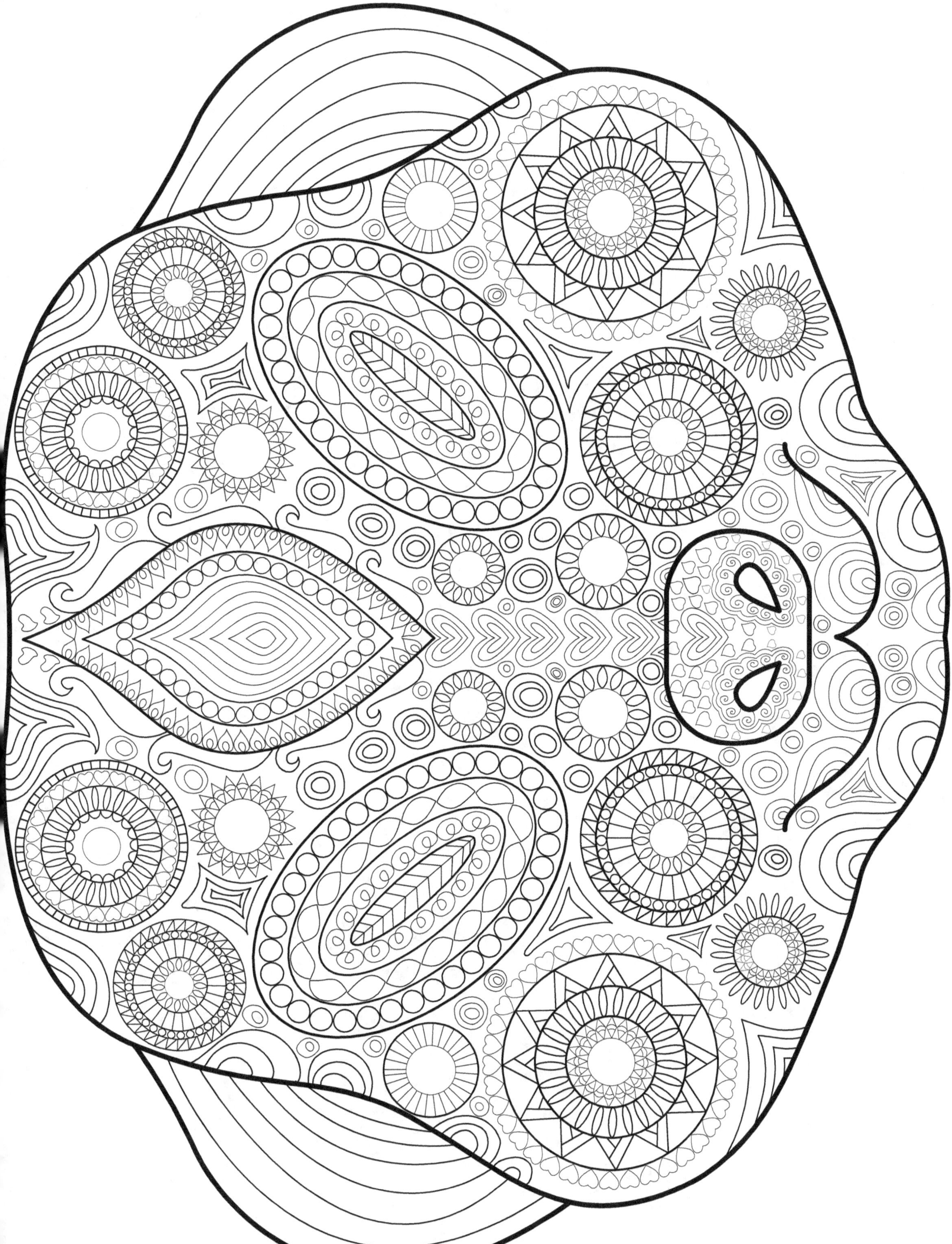

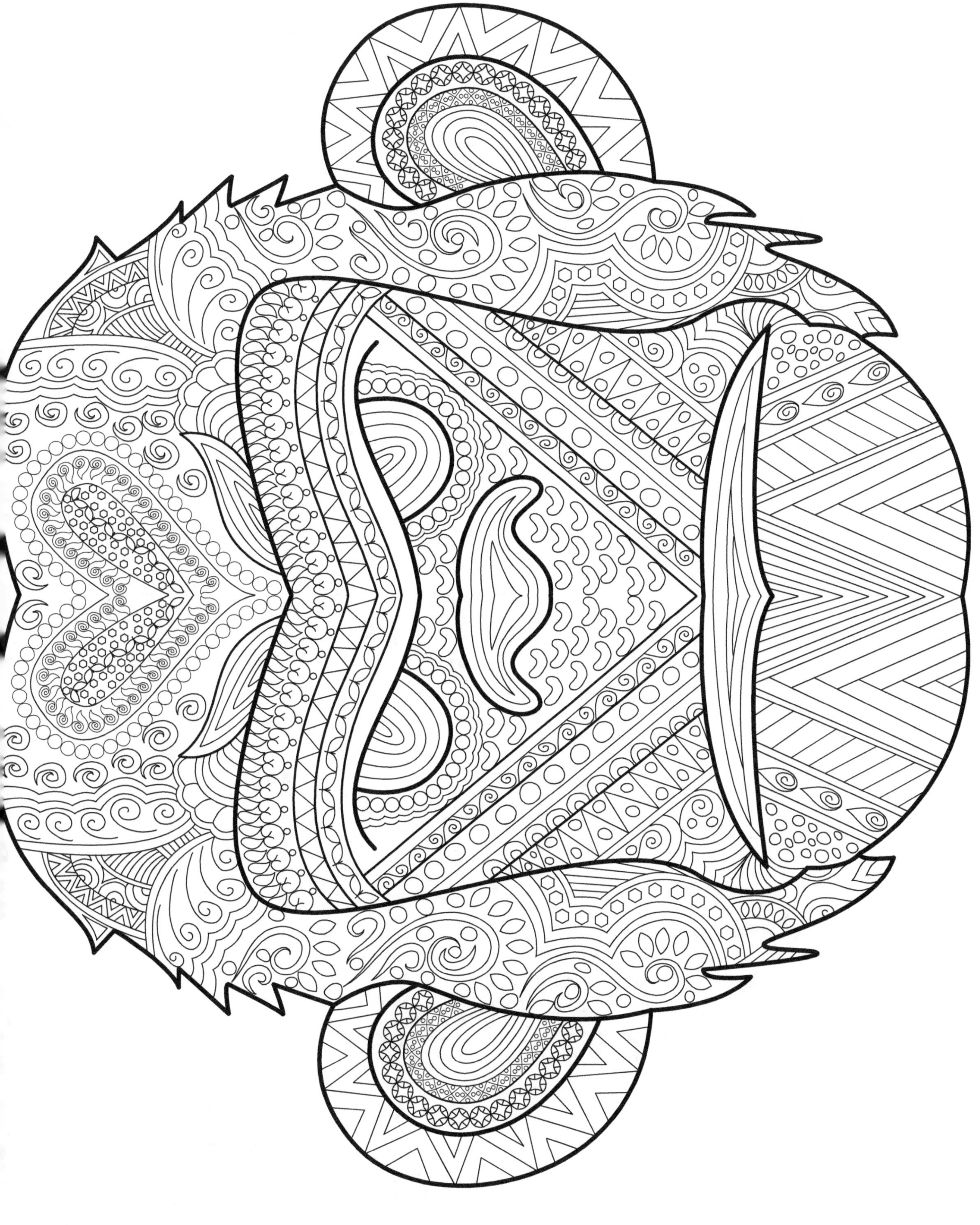

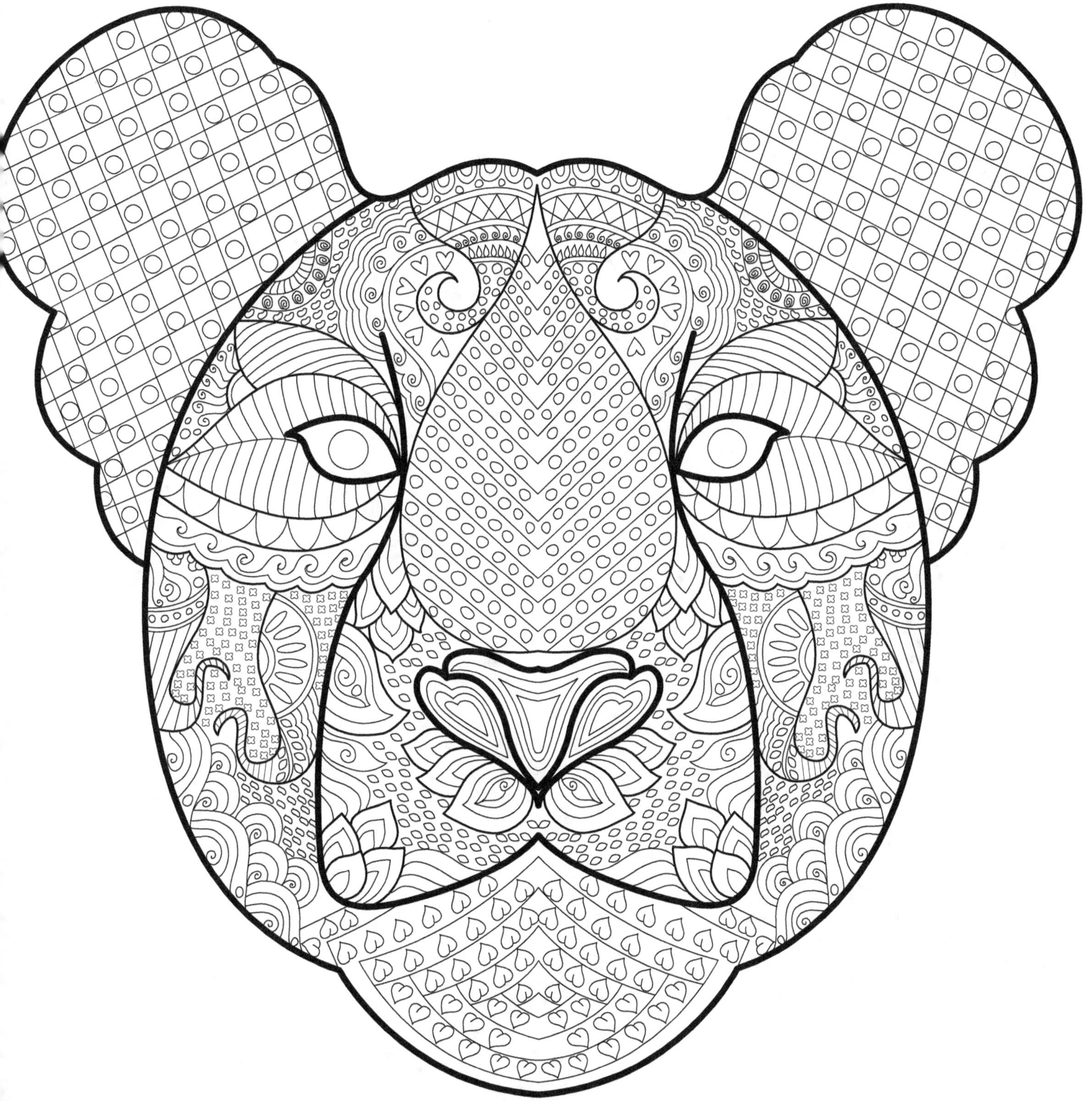

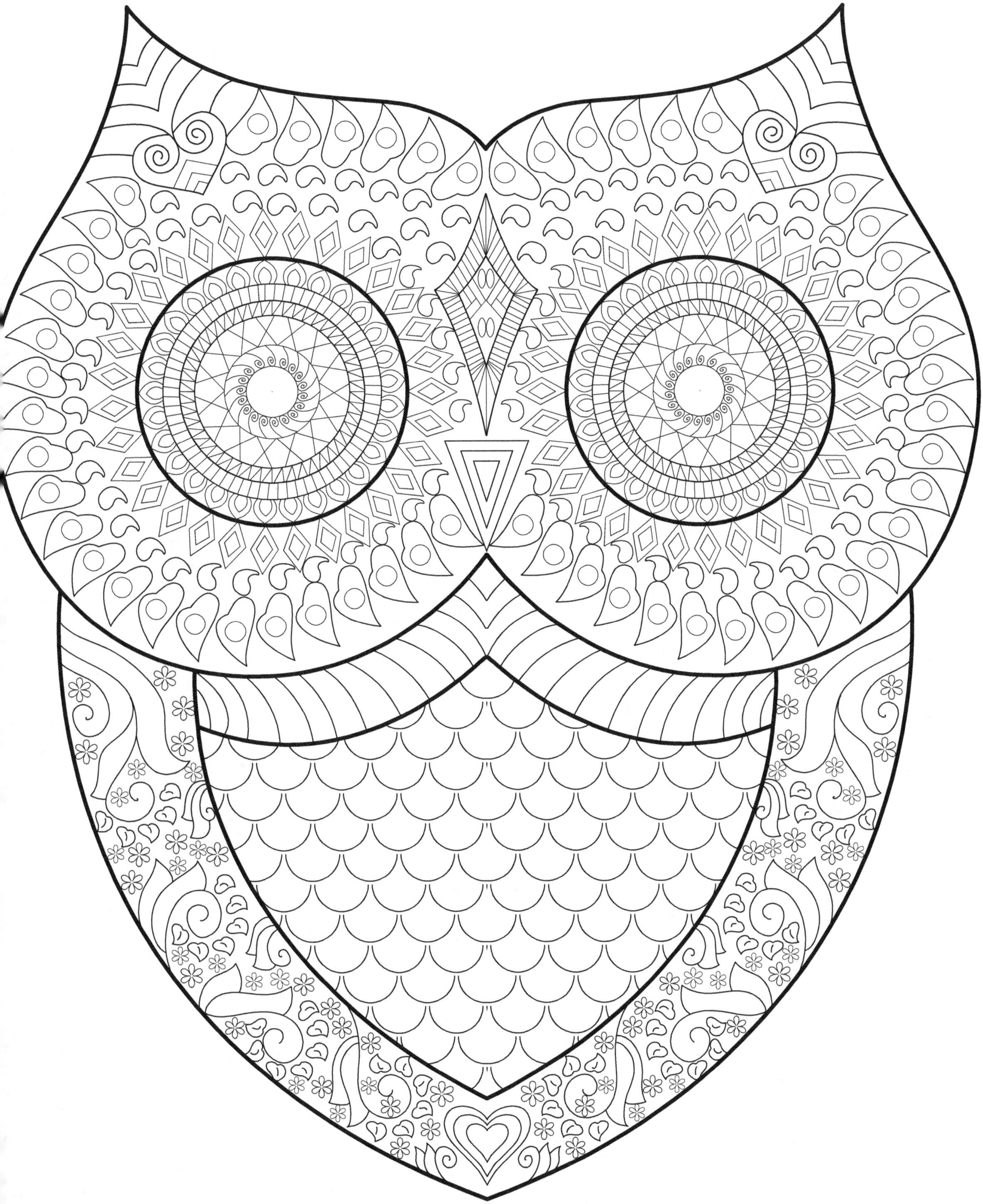

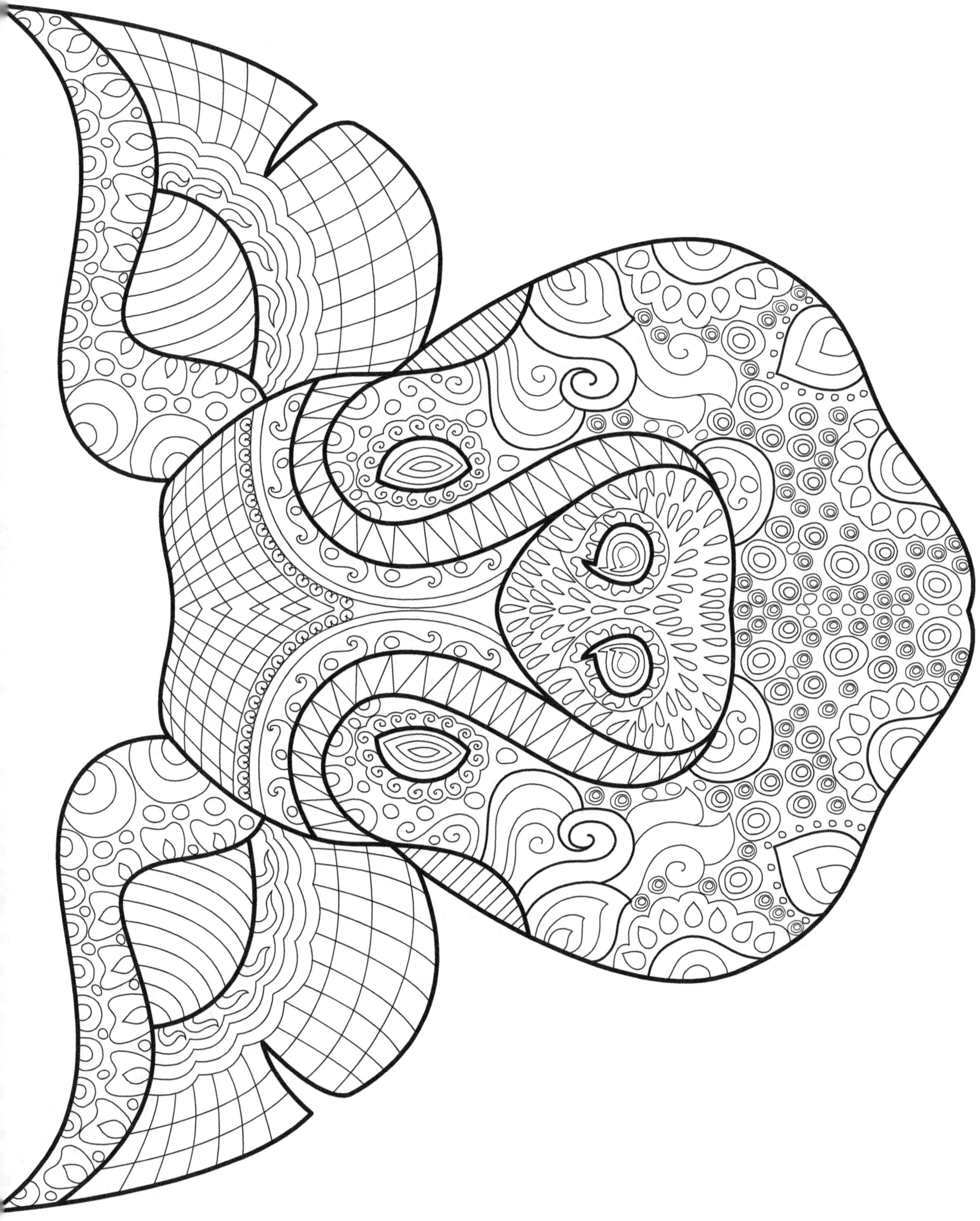

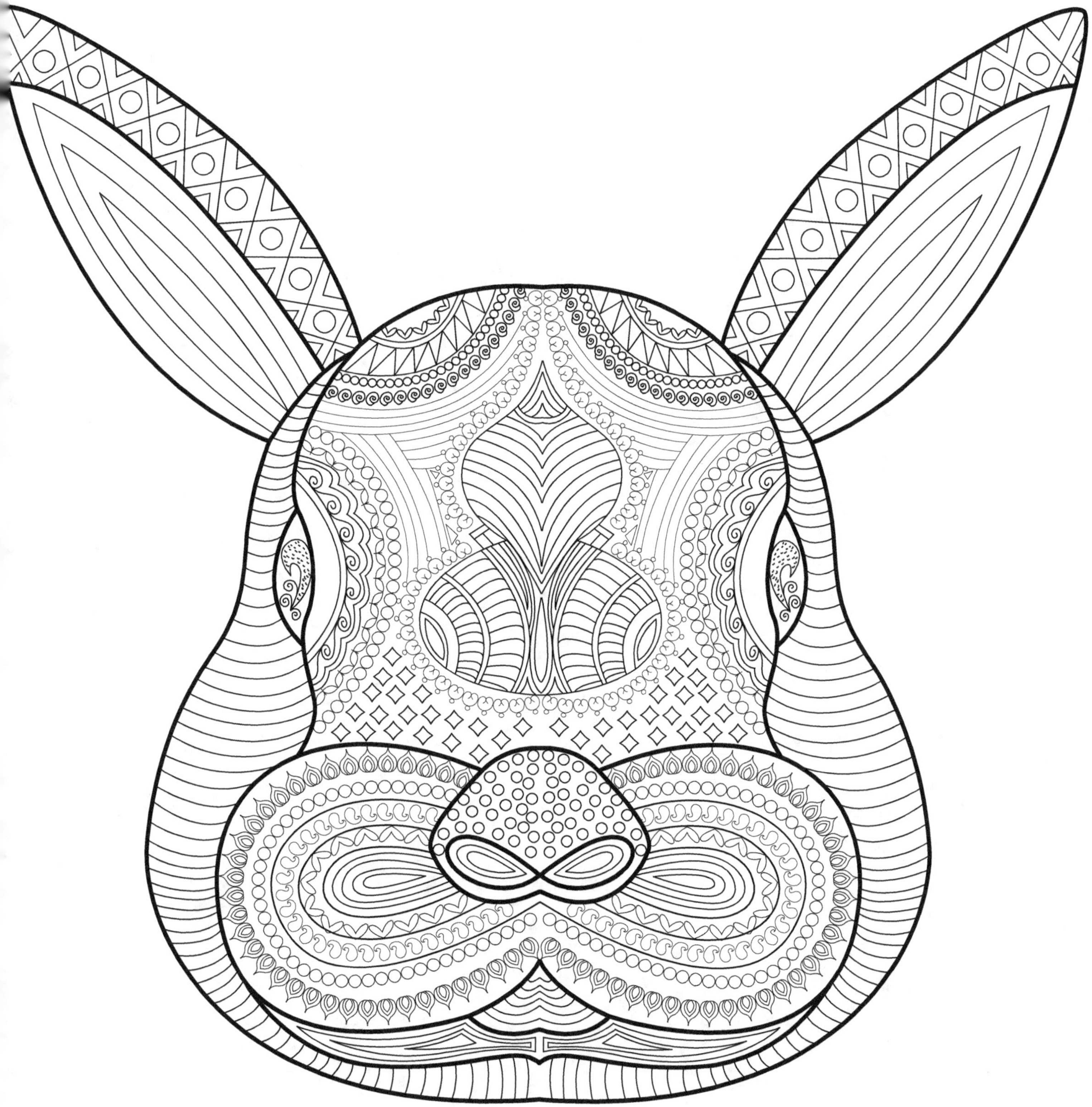

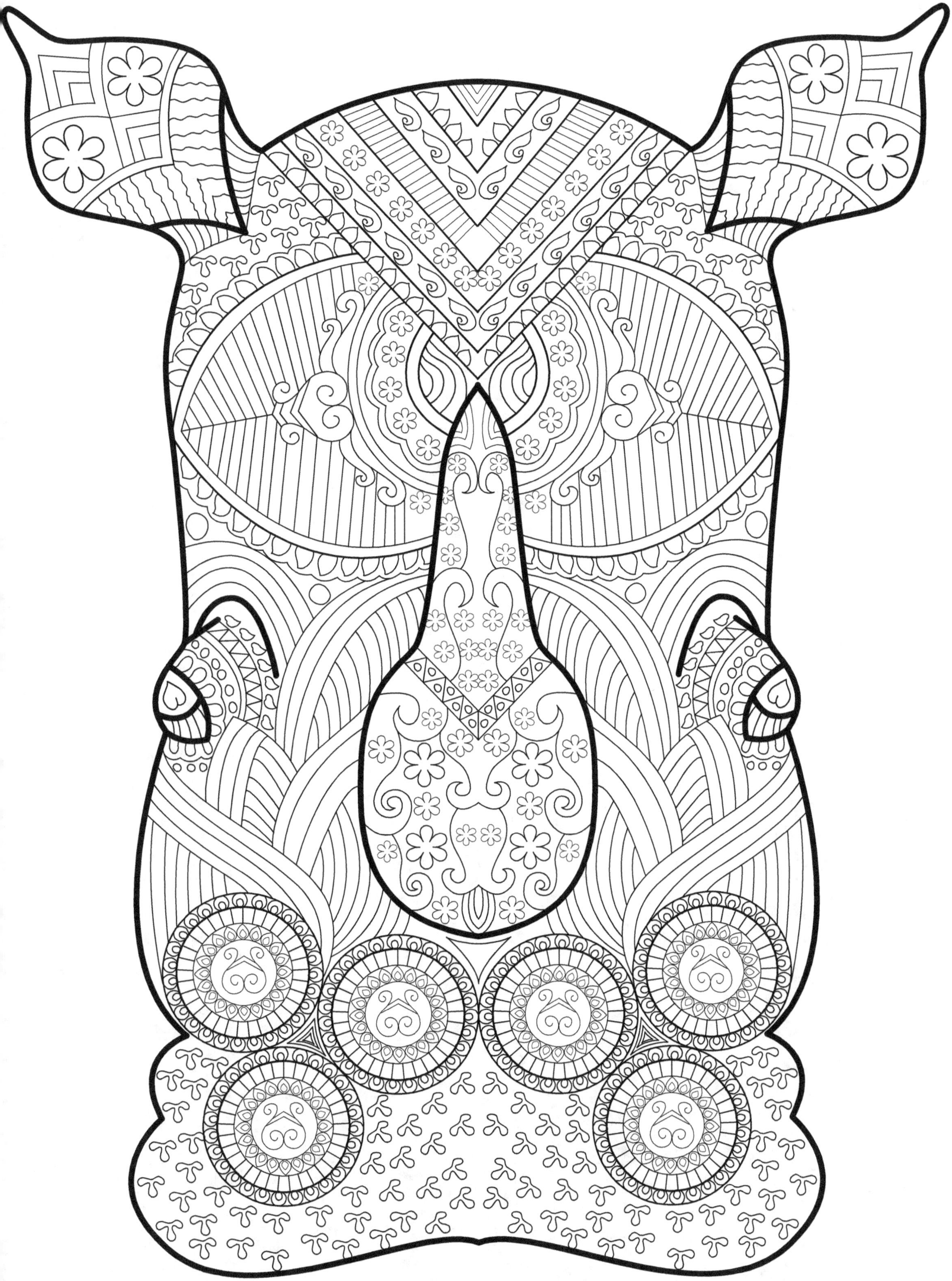

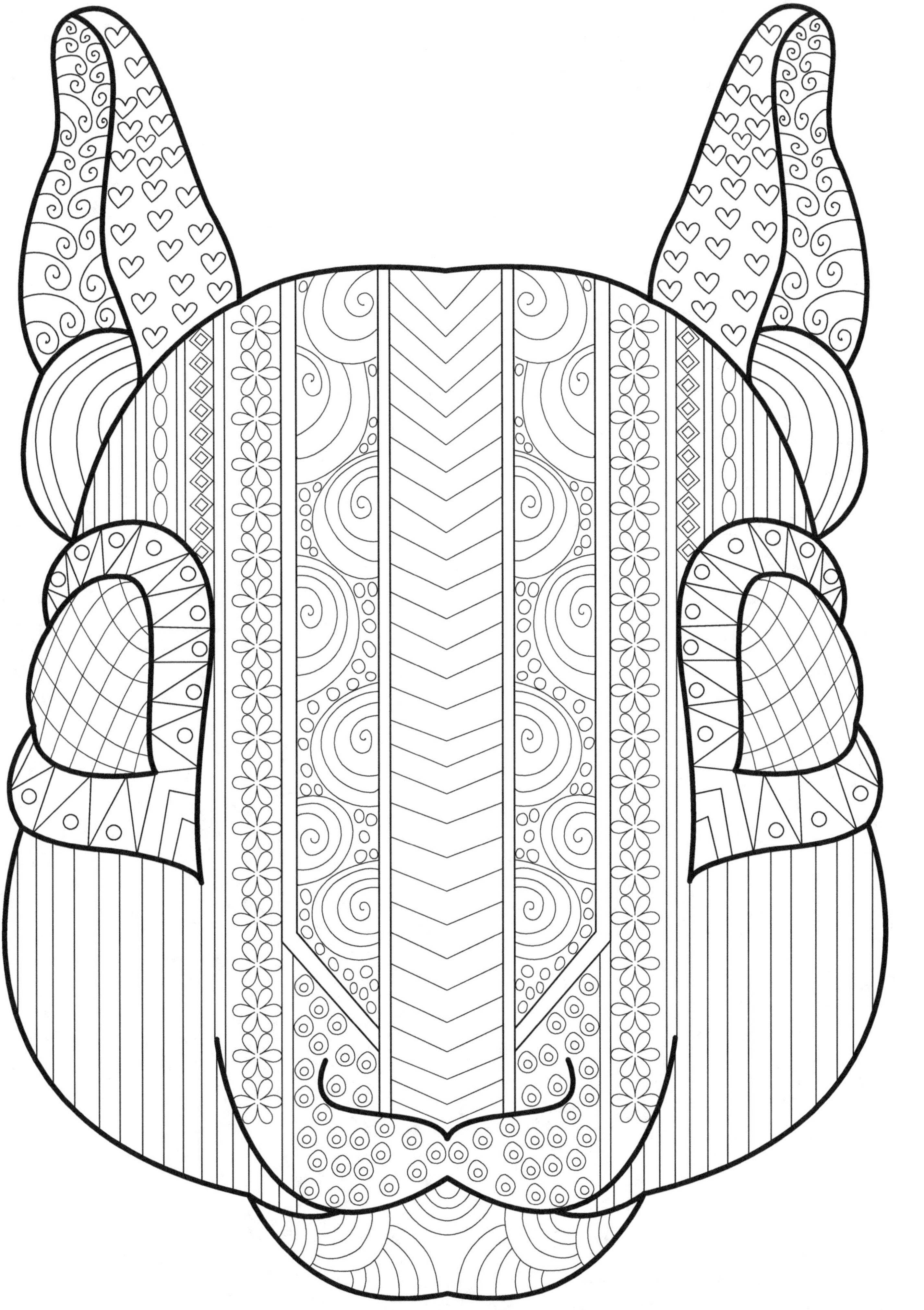

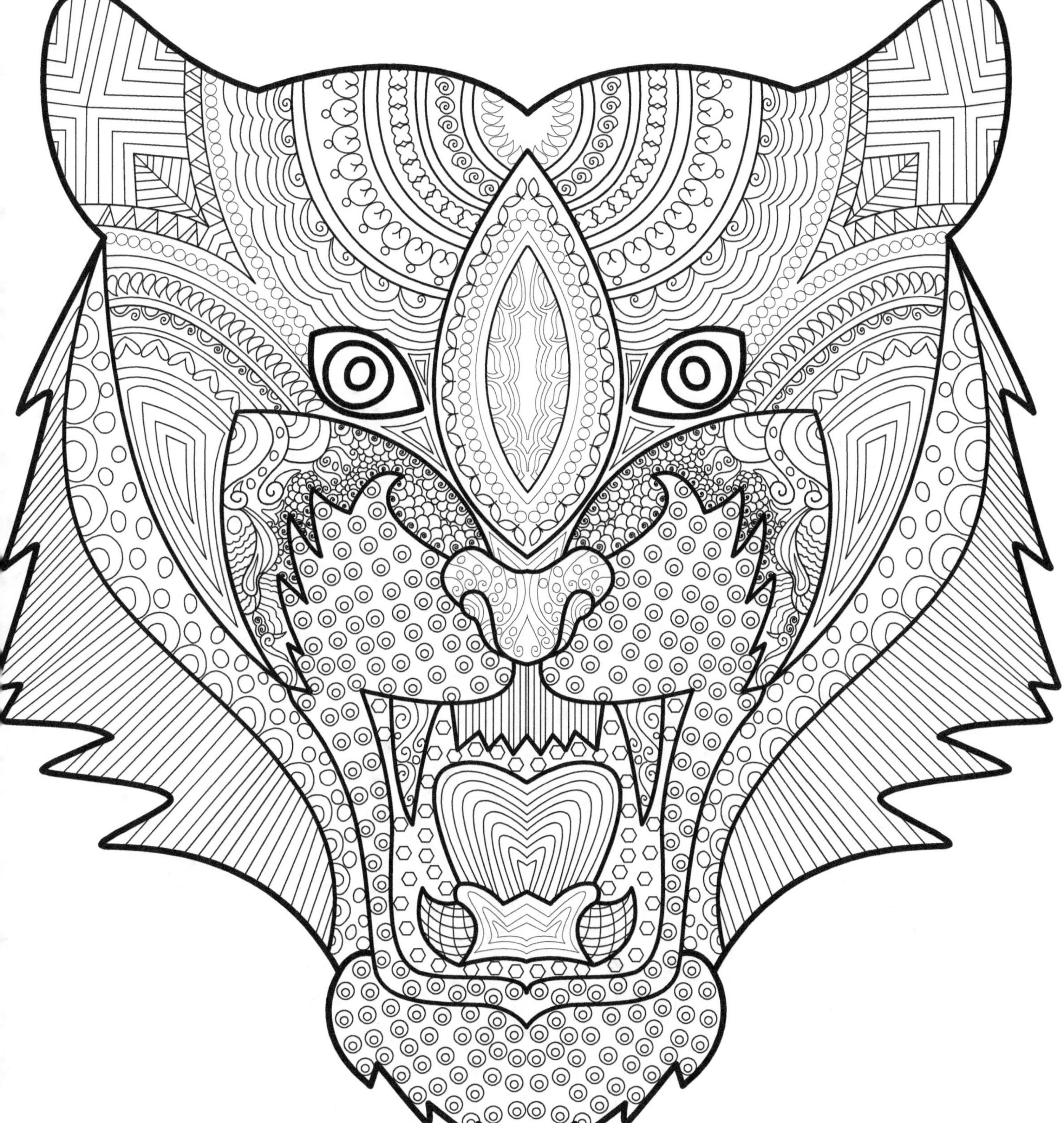

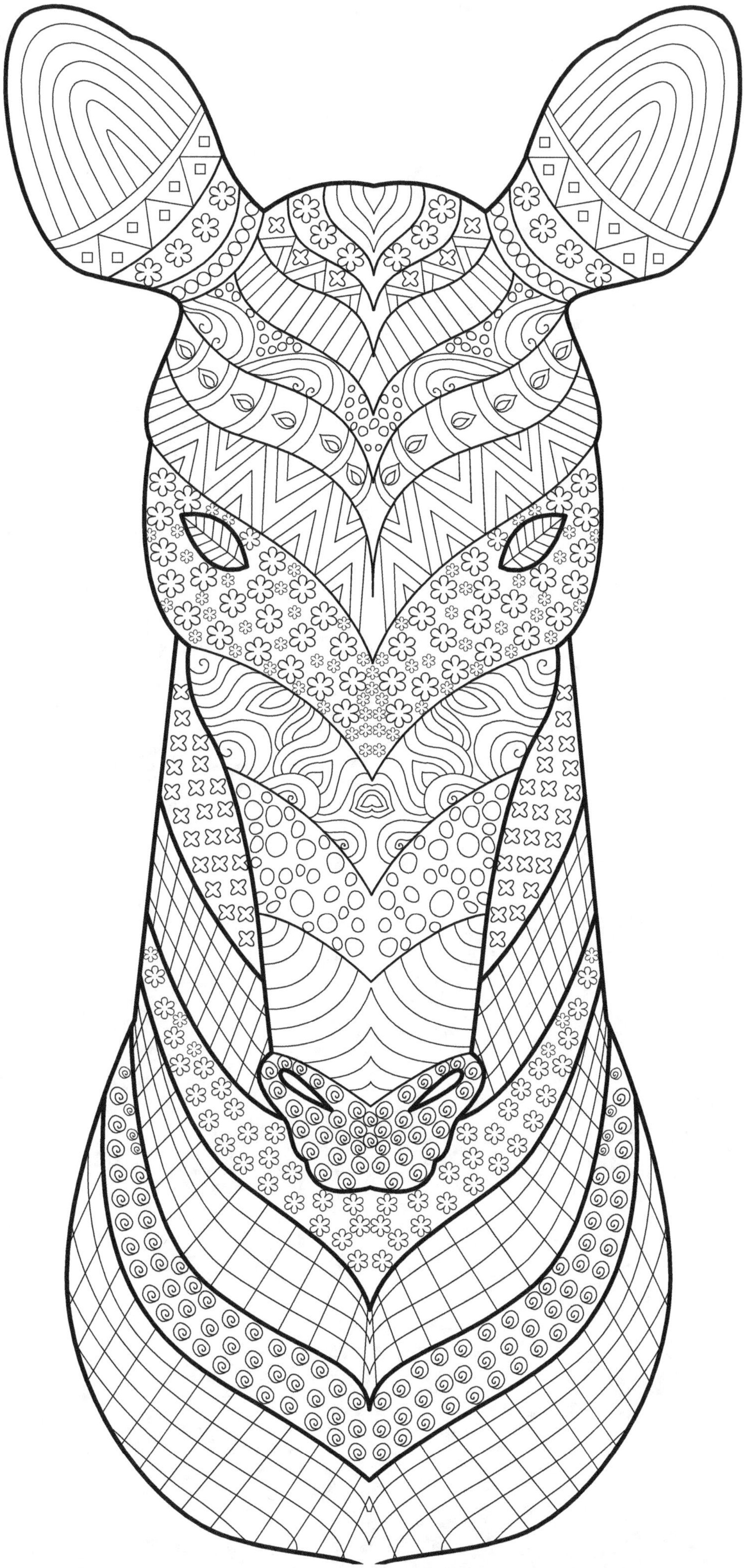

MAZE

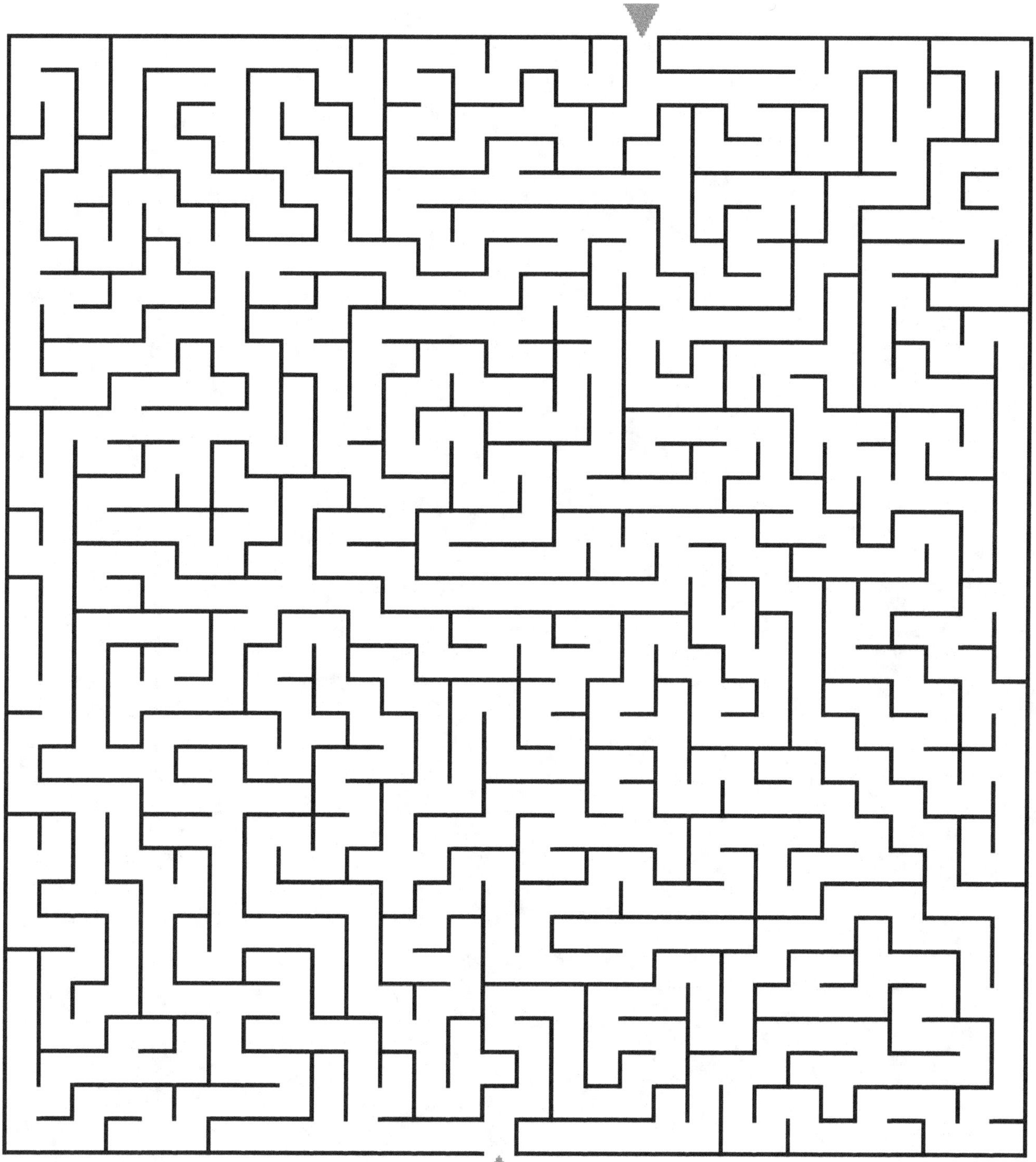

COLOR CHARTS

Solution

www.ingramcontent.com/pod-product-compliance
Lightning Source LLC
Chambersburg PA
CBHW081452220526
45466CB00008B/2610
9781690864189